ACOUSTIC GUITAR
PRIVATE LESSONS

ALTERNATE TUNINGS GUITAR ESSENTIALS

STRING LETTER

Publisher: David A. Lusterman

Editorial Director: Jeffrey Pepper Rodgers

Editor: Scott Nygaard

Managing Editor: Simone Solondz

Music Editor: Andrew DuBrock

Designer: Ray Larsen

Production Director: Ellen Richman

Production Coordinator: Judy Zimola

Marketing: Jen Fujimoto

Music Engraving: Andrew DuBrock

Cover Photo: Rory Earnshaw

Photographs: Crackerfarm (Duncan Sheik), Henry Diltz (David Crosby), Rory Earnshaw
(Steve James), Willie Floyd (Dylan Schorer), Anne Hamersky (Scott Nygaard), Chugrad
McAndrews (Teja Gerken), Sunny Reynolds (Paul Reisler), Richard Russell (Steve Baughman),
Patrick O'Connor (David Hamburger), Michael Wilson (David Wilcox), Irene Young (Al Petteway)

**STRING
LETTER**

Contents

Audio Track List

The complete set of audio tracks for the musical examples and songs in *Alternate Tunings Guitar Essentials* is available for free download at AcousticGuitar.com/ATGEAudio. Just add the tracks to your shopping cart and enter the discount code "ATGETracks12" during checkout to activate your free download.

Introduction

Alternate tunings have become so prevalent in recent years that standard tuning can really only be called *standard* in a few genres (jazz, bluegrass, classical) anymore. Acoustic blues, Celtic, contemporary folk, and rock guitarists are just as likely to put their guitars in an open or alternate tuning as in E A D G B E tuning. But many guitarists who find themselves intrigued by the sonorous possibilities available with alternate tunings are also overwhelmed by the sheer number of choices and variables that confront them when they start twisting their pegs. This lesson book will guide you down the path of alternate tunings, showing you how to begin and where you might go on your journey.

In Getting Started, Gary Joyner introduces you to the world of alternate tunings and the players who've pioneered them, while Paul Reisler tells you how to make sense of the basic open tunings and find the chords you need. In Common Tunings, *Acoustic Guitar* magazine's master teachers explore the most familiar open tunings with in-depth lessons that include exercises and songs to play in each tuning. In Further Explorations, you'll hear from such alternate-tuning avatars as David Crosby and Alex de Grassi and get tuner-twisting tips from masters like Martin Simpson and David Wilcox. You'll also find a few arrangements to play from three guitarists who explain how they discovered the tunings that have enriched and inspired their music. As you begin to explore, you'll want to refer to "60 Tunings (and the Artists Who Love Them)," an exhaustive list of tunings along with the artists and songs they're often associated with. And to help you prepare your instrument for these excursions, *Acoustic Guitar* magazine's gear guru, Teja Gerken, offers tips on setup and alternate-tuning gear.

So dive in and see why alternate tunings have become the new standard for creative guitarists of all stripes.

Scott Nygaard
Editor

Music Notation Key

The music in this book is written in standard notation and tablature. Here's how to read it.

STANDARD NOTATION

Standard notation is written on a five-line staff. Notes are written in alphabetical order from A to G.

The duration of a note is determined by three things: the note head, stem, and flag. A whole note (○) equals four beats. A half note (♩) is half of that: two beats. A quarter note (♩) equals one beat, an eighth note (♪) equals half of one beat, and a 16th note (♪) is a quarter beat (there are four 16th notes per beat).

The fraction (4/4, 3/4, 6/8, etc.) or c character shown at the beginning of a piece of music denotes the time signature. The top number tells you how many beats are in each measure, and the

bottom number indicates the rhythmic value of each beat (4 equals a quarter note, 8 equals an eighth note, 16 equals a 16th note, and 2 equals a half note). The most common time signature is 4/4, which signifies four quarter notes per measure and is sometimes designated with the symbol c (for common time). The symbol ¢ stands for cut time (2/2). Most songs are either in 4/4 or 3/4.

TABLATURE

In tablature, the six horizontal lines represent the six strings of the guitar, with the first string on the top and sixth on the bottom. The numbers refer to fret numbers on a given string. The notation and tablature in this book are designed to be used in tandem—refer to the notation to get the rhythmic information and note durations, and refer to the tablature to get the exact locations of the notes on the guitar fingerboard.

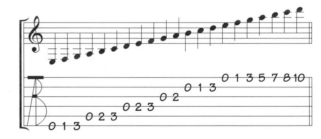

FINGERINGS

Fingerings are indicated with small numbers and letters in the notation. Fretting-hand fingering is indicated with 1 for the index finger, 2 the middle, 3 the ring, 4 the pinky, and T the thumb. Picking-hand fingering is indicated by i for the index finger, m the middle, a the ring, c the pinky, and p the thumb. Circled numbers indicate the string the note is played on. Remember that the fingerings indicated are only suggestions; if you find a different way that works better for you, use it.

CHORD DIAGRAMS

Chord diagrams show where the fingers go on the fingerboard. Frets are shown horizontally. The thick top line represents the nut. A Roman numeral to the right of a diagram indicates a chord played higher up the neck (in this case the top horizontal line is thin). Strings are shown as vertical lines. The line on the far left represents the sixth (lowest) string, and the line on the far right represents the first (highest) string. Dots show where the fingers go, and thick horizontal lines indicate barres. Numbers above the diagram are left-hand finger numbers, as used in standard notation. Again, the fingerings are only suggestions. An X indicates a string that should be muted or not played; 0 indicates an open string.

CAPOS

If a capo is used, a Roman numeral indicates the fret where the capo should be placed. The standard notation and tablature is written as if the capo were the nut of the guitar. For instance, a tune capoed anywhere up the neck and played using key-of-G chord shapes and fingerings will be written in the key of G. Likewise, open strings held down by the capo are written as open strings.

TUNINGS

Alternate guitar tunings are given from the lowest (sixth) string to the highest (first) string. For instance, D A D G B E indicates standard tuning with the bottom string dropped to D. Standard notation for songs in alternate tunings always reflects the actual pitches of the notes. Arrows underneath tuning notes indicate strings that are altered from standard tuning and whether they are tuned up or down.

VOCAL TUNES

Vocal tunes are sometimes written with a fully tabbed-out introduction and a vocal melody with chord diagrams for the rest of the piece. The tab intro is usually your indication of which strum or fingerpicking pattern to use in the rest of the piece. The melody with lyrics underneath is the melody sung by the vocalist. Occasionally, smaller notes are written with the melody to indicate the harmony part sung by another vocalist. These are not to be confused with cue notes, which are small notes that indicate melodies that vary when a section is repeated. Listen to a recording of the piece to get a feel for the guitar accompaniment and to hear the singing if you aren't skilled at reading vocal melodies.

ARTICULATIONS

There are a number of ways you can articulate a note on the guitar. Notes connected with slurs (not to be confused with ties) in the tablature or standard notation are articulated with either a hammer-on, pull-off, or slide. Lower notes slurred to higher notes are played as hammer-ons; higher notes slurred to lower notes are

played as pull-offs. While it's usually obvious that slurred notes are played as hammer-ons or pull-offs, an H or P is included above the tablature as an extra reminder.

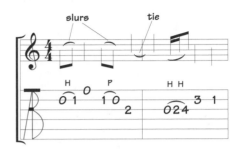

Slides are represented with a dash, and an S is included above the tab. A dash preceding a note represents a slide into the note from an indefinite point in the direction of the slide; a dash following a note indicates a slide off of the note to an indefinite point in the direction of the slide. For two slurred notes connected with a slide, you should pick the first note and then slide into the second.

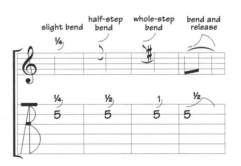

Bends are represented with upward curves, as shown in the next example. Most bends have a specific destination pitch—the number above the bend symbol shows how much the bend raises the string's pitch: $\frac{1}{4}$ for a slight bend, $\frac{1}{2}$ for a half step, 1 for a whole step.

Grace notes are represented by small notes with a dash through the stem in standard notation and with small numbers in the tab. A grace note is a very quick ornament leading into a note, most commonly executed as a hammer-on, pull-off, or slide. In the first example below, pluck the note at the fifth fret on the beat, then quickly hammer onto the seventh fret. The second example is executed as a quick pull-off from the second fret to the open string. In the third example, both notes at the fifth fret are played simultaneously (even though it appears that the fifth fret, fourth string, is to be played by itself), then the seventh fret, fourth string, is quickly hammered.

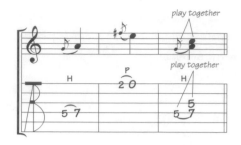

HARMONICS

Harmonics are represented by diamond-shaped notes in the standard notation and a small dot next to the tablature numbers. Natural harmonics are indicated with the text "Harmonics" or "Harm." above the tablature. Harmonics articulated with the right hand (often called artificial harmonics) include the text "R.H. Harmonics" or "R.H. Harm." above the tab. Right-hand harmonics are executed by lightly touching the harmonic node (usually 12 frets above the open string or fretted note) with the right-hand index finger and plucking the string with the thumb or ring finger or pick. For extended phrases played with right-hand harmonics, the fretted notes are shown in the tab along with instructions to touch the harmonics 12 frets above the notes.

REPEATS

One of the most confusing parts of a musical score can be the navigation symbols, such as repeats, D.S. al Coda, D.C. al Fine, To Coda, etc.

Repeat symbols are placed at the beginning and end of the passage to be repeated.

You should ignore repeat symbols with the dots on the right side the first time you encounter them; when you come to a repeat symbol with dots on the left side, jump back to the previous repeat symbol facing the opposite direction (if there is no previous symbol, go to the beginning of the piece). The next time you come to the repeat symbol, ignore it and keep going unless it includes instructions such as "Repeat three times."

A section will often have a different ending after each repeat. The example below includes a first and a second ending. Play until you hit the repeat symbol, jump back to the previous repeat symbol and play until you reach the bracketed first ending, skip the measures under the bracket and jump immediately to the second ending, and then continue.

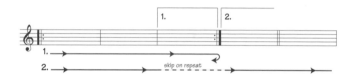

D.S. stands for dal segno or "from the sign." When you encounter this indication, jump immediately to the sign (𝄋). D.S. is usually accompanied by al Fine or al Coda. Fine indicates the end of a piece. A coda is a final passage near the end of a piece and is indicated with 𝄌. D.S. al Coda simply tells you to jump back to the sign and continue on until you are instructed to jump to the coda, indicated with To Coda 𝄌.

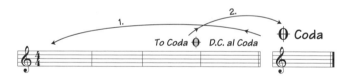

D.C. stands for da capo or "from the beginning." Jump to the top of the piece when you encounter this indication.

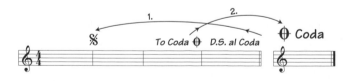

D.C. al Fine tells you to jump to the beginning of a tune and continue until you encounter the Fine indicating the end of the piece (ignore the Fine the first time through).

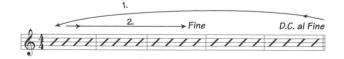

About the Teachers

STEVE BAUGHMAN

Steve Baughman is a San Francisco guitarist who loves guitar music with melody, especially Celtic and Appalachian music. He has one solo album, *A Drop of the Pure*, on his own Tall Trees record label (1522 29th Ave., San Francisco, CA 94122; [800] 649-4745) and he appears with Pierre Bensusan, Martin Simpson, and others on the Rounder Records compilation *Ramble to Cashel*. Baughman has also released two Mel Bay books, Celtic Guitar Method and Celtic Fingerstyle Solos. He is a partner in the San Francisco law firm of Baughman and Wang, where he practices primarily in the area of political asylum law. He has taught at the Swannanoa Gathering and can be reached at celticguitar.com.

DAVID HAMBURGER

David Hamburger is a guitarist, teacher, and writer who lives in Brooklyn, New York. He has toured with Salamander Crossing and Five Chinese Brothers and appeared on recent recordings by Chuck Brodsky and the Kennedys. A regular instructor at the National Guitar Summer Workshop, Hamburger has written three instruction books, including *The Dobro Workbook*. His latest solo recording is Indigo Rose, on Chester Records (songs. com).

STEVE JAMES

Steve James is a touring performer and recording artist based in Austin, Texas. He was born in New York, where he got caught up in the folk/blues/roots revival and started playing guitar as a teenager. To get closer to the music, he moved to Tennessee and played with Sam McGee, Furry Lewis, and many other master musicians. James' original music and arrangements for guitar, slide guitar, mandolin, and guitar-banjo can be heard on *Two Track Mind, American Primitive*, and *Art and Grit* (all on Antone's). He is a contributing editor for Acoustic Guitar magazine and is the author of the lesson book *Roots and Blues Fingerstyle Guitar* (String Letter Publishing). For more information, visit his web site at stevejames.com.

GARY JOYNER

Gary Joyner has worked and played as an acoustic guitarist and singer in restaurants, clubs, coffeehouses, and on concert stages and cruise ships. He teaches private students, clinics, and classes about acoustic guitar, fingerstyle guitar, guitar tunings, songwriting, music theory, performance, creativity, and harmonica. He also writes for guitar magazines such as *Acoustic Guitar*. He lives in St. Paul, Minnesota.

SCOTT NYGAARD

Scott Nygaard, *Acoustic Guitar* magazine's associate editor, is an accomplished guitarist with more than 25 years' experience. He has performed and recorded with such artists as

Laurie Lewis and Grant Street, Tim O'Brien and the O'Boys, David Grisman, and Jerry Douglas; released two albums, *No Hurry* and *Dreamer's Waltz*, on Rounder Records; and been nominated for a number of Grammy awards for his work on other artists' CDs. He lives in San Francisco and performs with the Quirks and singer Chris Webster. His instructional video *Bluegrass Lead Guitar* was recently released by Stefan Grossman's Guitar Workshop.

AL PETTEWAY

Al Petteway is the coordinator for the Swannanoa Gathering's Guitar Week and teaches private lessons in his home in Takoma Park, Maryland. He has won more than three dozen awards from the Washington Area Music Association and the Maryland State Arts Council. *Racing Hearts*, his sixth recording and first entirely collaborative effort with his wife, Amy White, was released in February 2000 on the Fairewood label. They are currently working on a duo guitar recording for the Groovemasters series on Solid Air Records. Petteway can be reached at fairewood.com.

PAUL REISLER

Cofounder of the acclaimed chamber-folk acoustic ensemble Trapezoid, Paul Reisler is a composer, songwriter, performer, and teacher. He has toured throughout North America, Japan, Asia, and Africa over the past two decades, performing in more than 2,000 concerts, workshops, and festivals. In concert Reisler performs on hammered dulcimer and guitar, instruments he's been exploring for more than 35 years. He teaches at songwriting workshops across North America, and his latest instrumental album, *Birth of a River* (Azure, PO Box 38, Washington, VA 22747), is a collaborative effort with Bobby Read.

DYLAN SCHORER

Dylan Schorer was *Acoustic Guitar*'s music editor from 1994 to 1999. He won the 1993 fingerpicking contest at the Telluride Bluegrass Festival, and he performs throughout the San Francisco Bay Area, accompanying various songwriters and playing solo. He currently plays and records in the Celtic ensemble Logan's Well with guitarist Steve Baughman and vocalist Carleen Duncan.

An Introduction to Alternate Tunings

GARY JOYNER

Musicians have been experimenting with tunings ever since the first strands of gut were stretched across a soundbox. Exactly when those boxes came to be guitars is open to debate, as is their national lineage, but it's safe to say that what we call six-string "standard" tuning came into play somewhere around 1800. Its popularity is due to the fact that five different root notes are available in each position and that common chords can be fingered easily. Still, one wonders who first had the audacity to decide that this tuning is the "standard." Other tuning options are endless, and they offer tantalizing possibilities—an expanded palette of colors, new environments for rhythmic development, and the opportunity to escape from tiresome patterns. Alternate tunings are particularly seductive on high-quality acoustic guitars, with their deep resonance and responsiveness. For all these reasons, more guitarists than ever are twiddling their tuning pegs these days, from solo fingerstyle players to folk singer-songwriters to rock bands.

Those who do start exploring alternate tunings, though, quickly find out that leaving standard tuning can be more than a little confusing, even frustrating. To help you get started, I'll walk you through some alternate tuning basics and then share the insights and advice of seven master guitarist-composers who've made tunings an integral part of their music.

HISTORY

Various claims have been put forth regarding the derivation of alternate tunings. For example, open G-major tuning (from the lowest string to the highest, D G D G B D) has been traced by some to the slack-key style of Hawaii and by others to Germany. We know that altered tunings were popular with many early American blues guitarists. Robert Johnson and Blind Willie Johnson tuned their guitars to open chords in order to have a solid low root note to pound with their thumb and to facilitate bottleneck slide styles.

The fingerstyle explosion of the 1960s that began with John Fahey and Leo Kottke was in part a result of open tunings. Across the Atlantic, the tuning phenomenon was rooted in a fusion of Great Britain's traditional music with American blues. Fingerstylists Martin Carthy, John Renbourn, Bert Jansch, Davey Graham, and Martin Simpson were outstanding players in the movement. Simpson maintains that many cutting-edge guitar tunings originated on the American banjo. D A D G A D, commonly considered to be an invention of Davey Graham in the 1960s, contains the same intervals as the five-string banjo's older traditional "sawmill tuning," G D G C D. The 1980s heralded a further leap into tuning creativity with the instrumental music of Pierre Bensusan, Alex de Grassi, Will Ackerman, and the late Michael Hedges.

Starting in the late '60s, songwriting icons Joni Mitchell and David Crosby affected the course of all popular music with their idiosyncratic tunings, while in England, the late Nick Drake created an intimate, tuning-based style that has quietly influenced several generations of guitarist-songwriters. Today, you can hear the legacy of these artists in the contemporary folk-rock of David Wilcox, Duncan Sheik, Ani DiFranco, and many other singer-songwriters.

The reason most players venture from standard tuning is to gain access to the sound of open ringing strings.

Introduction

Even in genres more grounded in standard tuning, there are notable innovators. Italian guitarist Beppe Gambetta carved out a niche for himself by using alternate tunings for American and European traditional music in the context of flatpicking, while guitarist-composers like Andrew York use tunings in their nylon-string creations.

Tune-up: Standard **TRACK 2**

LOST AND FOUND

Let's start our exploration of tunings by defining some terms. Strictly speaking, an "open tuning" is one in which the open strings are tuned to a simple chord, while "altered tunings" draw on other harmonic possibilities. The two terms are, however, often used interchangeably.

The reason most players venture from standard tuning is to gain access to the sound of ringing open strings, and to be able to reach notes and intervals that are impossible in standard tuning. "What I love most about altered tunings is that they're a fresh start," says singer-songwriter David Wilcox, "sort of a beginner's mind. It's like picking up a new musical instrument that no one's ever seen before." He speaks often of the wonderful mystery and chaos of getting lost on the guitar.

Martin Simpson, a master teacher and player of alternate tunings and slide guitar, clarifies his own approach to the concept of getting lost. "If you're milling about the instrument in an unconscious fashion, you're not even going to know when you're lost. You have to become conscious to get lost, conscious of what an open tuning is in simple theoretical terms, how it relates to standard tuning and other open tunings. Then you will have more fun being lost."

Despite the fingerboard disorientation they may cause, alternate tunings in fact allow you to understand music theory in a new, graphic way. Chord structure can be easier to visualize on the fretboard in an altered tuning, as you'll see in the examples below.

A few technical considerations to keep in mind when you're working with tunings: If you use light-gauge strings for tunings that lower pitches below standard, chances are you'll run into some frustrations with string buzzing and rattle. All the players I've talked to use medium-gauge or heavier strings for altered tunings. Martin Simpson replaces the first string of a medium set (normally a .013) with an even heavier .015. He finds it reduces unwanted noise and provides support for his slide. String breakage is a potential problem when you're continually tuning up and down. It can be minimized by allowing enough slack for some extra windings when you install strings and by changing strings often. And it helps if you can dedicate at least one guitar to altered tunings. For more advice on these issues, see "Strings, Setup, and Gizmos for Alternate Tunings" in the Reference section.

A chromatic electronic tuner (which can "read" all pitches—not just the E A D G B E of standard tuning) will make navigation through tunings easier to accomplish. If you are working with other musicians, a tuner is particularly useful because the changing tension on the guitar neck will affect the pitch of all the strings.

STANDARD TUNING

The standard six-string guitar tuned E A D G B E first appeared in the late 1700s, but its evolution spanned more than 30 centuries. According to Maurice Summerfeld (*The Classical Guitar*, Ashley Mark 1991), the first guitar-shaped instrument was found on a Hittite archaelogical object that dates from 1400 BC, and the word *guitar* is derived from two Persian words, *char* (four) and *tar* (string). In the 1500s the two most popular guitarlike instruments were the vihuela and the four-course guitar, both of which demonstrated the hourglasslike guitar shape, as opposed to the rounder lute. The vihuela had six double courses and was tuned G C F A D G, while the four-course guitar was tuned C F A D, the same as the middle four strings of the vihuela. Both the lute and the vihuela gradually became less popular, especially when the four-course guitar's tuning was raised a whole step to D G B E and a lower fifth course (A) was added. The addition of the fifth string is often credited to the Spanish poet and musician Vicente Espinel (1551–1624). Most experts agree that the sixth string was added in the late 1700s. The German luthier Jakob August Otto is often credited as the first builder of a guitar with six single strings, adding the low E around 1790, but it appears that six-single-string guitars were being made in Italy decades before that.

—*Scott Nygaard*

Alternate tuning enthusiasts love to talk about how their guitars speak to them. It's almost like voodoo. As you experiment with the ideas presented here, I think you will find the same thing happening. Ideas leap from the guitar so quickly that remembering them becomes a problem. A small tape recorder is indispensable, although retrieval of information can be clumsy. Some sort of written notation is desirable.

TUNING NAMES AND NOTATION

First you need to be able to recall the tuning itself. Keeping track of the notes you've tuned each string to is one good way. Standard tuning is E A D G B E, starting with the sixth string. Some players, including Joni Mitchell, like to name the note of the sixth string and then use numbers to describe the tuning for each consecutive string. Standard tuning would be E-5 5 5 4 5: tune the sixth string to E and then fret it at the fifth fret to tune the fifth string; fret the fifth string at the fifth fret to tune the fourth string; and so on. One letter name and five numbers will thus describe a six-string tuning. Open-D tuning (D A D F♯ A D) would be notated as D-7 5 4 3 5.

It is useful to be aware of each tuning in terms of its chordal intervals. If you think of E as the root of standard tuning, you could describe it as R 4 ♭7 ♭3 5 R (R for root). This method will help you to understand the tuning, as Martin Simpson suggested. Standard tuning is actually a voicing of an Em11 chord. You will also begin to see that some seemingly unrelated tunings consist of identical intervals. D♯ G♯ C♯ F♯ A♯ D♯ appears to be a bizarre tuning until you realize that it's R 4 ♭7 ♭3 5 R, exactly the same as standard tuning (tuned down a half step).

"What I love most about altered tunings is that they're a fresh start, sort of a beginner's mind."
—David Wilcox

When it comes to notating melodies and arrangements, there's no escaping the value of tablature. It is simply too hard for most players to relate standard music notation to all the variables of tunings. Tab allows you to quickly and easily write the fret number on the appropriate string without worrying about what note you're playing. Don't forget to write the tuning you're using at the beginning of the tablature.

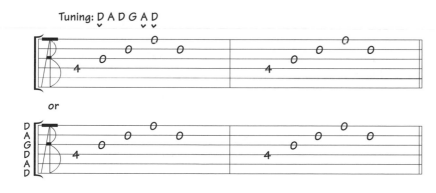

Chord grids like these provide a handy, visual way to write chord shapes:

The numeric notation system made popular on the Internet is also very handy. It consists of six numbers, one indicating which fret is held down on each string. A first-position D major chord in standard tuning, for example, is written x00232. The x is the muted sixth string, the 0's are open strings, and the numbers tell you where to fret strings three, two, and one.

Tune-up:
Dropped D

"People say they are overwhelmed by the possibilities on guitar. Go to an open tuning and explore a small piece of it."

—Martin Simpson

FIRST STEPS

The tuning that David Crosby jokingly calls "the first step down the road to ruin" is merely a matter of lowering the sixth string from E to D. It's known as dropped-D tuning. To get there, finger string six at the seventh fret and lower the resulting pitch until it matches the open fifth string. Crosby says that this is as far into the realm of altered tunings as the Byrds ever flew. D chords now have a root at the bottom. Fingerpickers can create a rich and solid alternating bass on open strings, making it easy to play melody and improvised lines on top. The low D can also work in any chord that already contains the open fourth string. Otherwise you will need to compensate for the lowered sixth string by fretting it two frets higher than you would in standard tuning. This is usually not a big problem, even with barre chords--especially if you are able to use the thumb of your fretting hand. Be sure to experiment widely to see what various chords sound like with that D on the bottom-—a G chord with a fifth in the bass, B♭ with a third in the bass, A with a fourth in the bass, and so on. The low D can provide an effective pedal tone, an unchanging note that continues under a progression of chords.

Next, drop the open first string to D by matching it to the second string fretted at the third fret. Now you're in what's commonly called double dropped-D tuning. It offers a reachable unison possibility between the first string and the second string fretted three frets higher. Remember that you now have two altered strings to manage when you finger chords, but strings two through five are still "normal." The first-position A-major shape moved up to the seventh fret gives you a rich D chord:

D
001230
VII

You are combining part of a fifth-position D barre chord with available open strings provided by the tuning. Strum through the chord, one string at a time. Notice the "melodic curve" that magically happens as you strum across the strings. And notice that some strings play octaves or unisons of each other, a significant attraction to alternate tunings. If you play a first-position E-major shape at the fourth fret, for example, you'll have a G-major chord with the fifth in the bass:

G/D
023100
IV

Add the sixth string fretted at the fifth fret (I use my left thumb), and you have the root, G, in the bass:

G
T23100
IV

Tune-up:
Double Dropped D

There are other delights to be found in even this modest tuning. Take time to search them out.

Bring the first string back up to E and lower the fifth string from A to G to get G6 tuning, D G D G B E (or 5 R 5 R 3 6). Match the open fifth string to the already retuned sixth string fingered at fret five. The first four strings are in standard tuning with all our familiar chord forms available. The only difference is that you have G and D bass notes on open strings. Stop strings one, two, and three at the third fret and you have a G-minor chord with the root on the open fifth string and the fifth on the open sixth string:

Tune-up: G6

Gm
x00111

Hold the Gm while you play a bass-line scale underneath it:

Ex. 1

Those open bass strings are very handy! Alex de Grassi, a fingerstyle and alternate tuning visionary who has inspired many guitarists to stray from standard tuning, recalls the first time he took the step of lowering the fifth string to G. "I realized I could do whatever I want with tuning!"

THREE BASIC OPEN TUNINGS

Now bring the first string down to D again to arrive at G major: D G D G B D, or 5 R 5 R 3 5. Improvise a melody up and down the full length of a single string of your choice while you strum the open chord. Try hammering and pulling off individual strings. Pluck any open string and hammer it at the third fret followed by the next higher string played open. Blues licks will leap out at you. Strings three and five are octaves—fret them both at the same fret up and down the fretboard. The same relationship applies to strings four and six. Use your index finger to barre all six strings at the fifth and seventh frets, and you will be playing C and D major chords, the IV and V chords in the key of G. You can make that V chord a dominant seventh, D7, with a root in the bass, by fretting 0x7577.

Tune-up: Open G

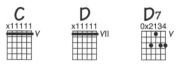

C   **D**   **D7**
x11111   x11111   0x2134

The landscape isn't entirely unfamiliar. Remember that strings two, three, and four are still in standard tuning. All familiar chord forms will apply on those strings. But now they live in a new neighborhood. An Am played on strings two, three, and four will still be an Am, and so on.

G-major tuning is one of the three seminal open-chord tunings. The two others are C major (C G C G C E) and D major (D A D F# A D). The majority of creative tuning alterations are derivations of these three. When you realize this and realize that the three tunings have distinct similarities, the apparently overwhelming scope begins to narrow. Consider the chord intervals in the tunings. G major is 5 R 5 R 3 5, D major is R 5 R 3 5 R, and C major is R 5 R 5 R 3. Notice that every one of them includes the series R 5 R 3.

In G it's on the middle four strings, surrounded by two fifths. In D it's on the lowest set of four adjacent strings with a 5 R on top. In C it's on top with a R 5 below. The R 5 R 3 series will have the same internal relationship no matter which strings it occupies. Chord shapes, bass lines, melodies, and licks learned on the string series will all be transferable to the other tunings.

We have arrived at the essence of Martin Simpson's approach to tunings. He reduces it further by disregarding the third. "Almost all open tunings will contain root-fifth-root and something additional," he explains. "The string set grouping will depend on the tuning you're in. Root-fifth-root is the essence of rock 'n' roll. It also is a beautiful package to play scales, to learn bass lines. People say they are overwhelmed by the possibilities on guitar. Go to an open tuning and explore a small piece of it. Learn where the intervals are within that root-fifth-root."

Understanding Open Tunings

PAUL REISLER

A student in one of my workshops once referred to playing in open tunings as the "hunter and gatherer's guitar method." You play around with a tuning until you find something you like and throw it in your bag. Then you play around some more until you have something to go with it. Pretty soon you have a pretty interesting musical salad. It's a fun way to play—a bit of a walk in the woods, not too mentally or physically taxing. It's fine until you have to play in a different key, improvise, or perform in a particular style. Then you're lost without a compass. Unless you know where you are going, it's easy to let the music lose direction and turn into a kind of musical wallpaper. Good music is all about tension and release: the tension moves the music forward toward release (or resolution). Music without tension can be pretty, but it has no movement. It's great in an elevator where you are already on the move.

I've been playing in many different open and altered guitar tunings for over 35 years now, and I've got to admit that I was a hunter and gatherer for many of them. About ten years ago I noticed that I wasn't wandering around so much anymore, that I seemed to know where I was going. I realized that I had come to an understanding of how the different tunings related to each other. A couple of years later it all fell into place when I was talking with one of my favorite players, Martin Simpson. He said that in his mind, the three most common major tunings, C, G, and D, are related to each other. I got out some paper and made some fingerboard charts of these three tunings, as well as the minor tunings, the suspended tunings (D A D G A D, D G D G C D), and a number of what I thought were oddball tunings. I put the different tunings into categories and realized that each new tuning was merely a variation of one I already knew. There were whole families of tunings that were just transpositions or small alterations of one another. I decided to put all of this into a system so I could teach it to people and understand it better myself.

In this lesson we'll look at the three major open tunings (in which the open strings form a chord) and learn how to improvise and transpose single-line melodies in them. The whole concept is based on having a visual map so you can find your way through the aural landscape. While you can wander around until you eventually get where you want to go, it's much more efficient to have a map.

THREE COMMON TUNINGS

On the next page, you'll find fretboard charts for three major tunings: C, G, and D. The numbers in the charts refer to the degrees of the scale in each key. In C tuning, for example, C is 1 or do, D is 2 or re, E is 3 or mi, etc. Music is a system of relationships, and you'll understand it a lot better if you think in terms of these relationships rather than getting stuck on the actual names of the notes. Notice that the distance from one note of the scale to the next is not always the same. Sometimes it's one fret, sometimes two. It's this particular pattern of half steps and whole steps that makes up the relationships of the major scale.

While you can wander around until you eventually get where you want to go, it's much more efficient to have a map.

Introduction   TRACK 8

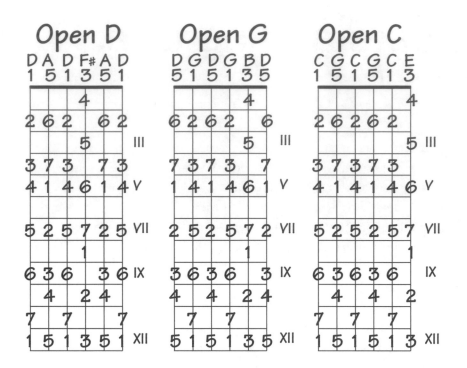

Spend some time looking at these patterns and notice what they have in common. Compare the C tuning and the G tuning. Do you see how the patterns of the notes relate to each other? The numbers are the same in G tuning as they are in C tuning except that the whole pattern is moved one string down (toward the bass side of the instrument). Now compare the G and D tunings. This time the pattern is shifted down one more string.

As you can see, in all three tunings most of the scale tones are played on the open strings and the second, fourth, and fifth frets. In each tuning, a few oddball notes are played on the open string and the first, third, and fifth frets. The string that supplies the oddball notes is always tuned to the third of the scale: in C tuning, it's the first string (E), in G the second string (B), and in D the third string (F♯).

Put your guitar in C tuning—C G C G C E, from low to high. The bottom three strings are tuned down, and the second goes up a half step to C. Play the open strings and listen to how wonderfully fat that C-major chord sounds. With the fretboard chart in front of you, try improvising a single-line melody using the open strings, second, fourth, and fifth frets for all but the first string, which you play open and fretted at the first, third, and fifth frets. Improvise for a while until you feel comfortable. Have fun with it, and don't try to play chords yet, just a simple melodic line against the drone of the open strings. Since you don't need to hold down the other notes of the chord with your fingers, you can really focus on getting a clear melodic sound out of the notes. You can affect the sound of the melody by adding vibrato and bends. Notice how certain notes create more tension against the drone.

Next, find a short phrase you like and repeat it until you can play it easily, without stumbling. Make up your own melody or try playing the melody written out in Example 1: the beginning of the traditional favorite "The Water Is Wide."

Tune-up:
Open C

Retune your guitar to G (D G D G B D) and play the same melody:

Tune-up:
Open G

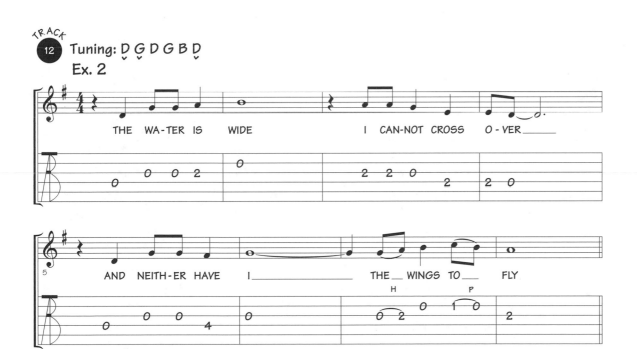

Tune-up:
Open D

TRACK 13

Notice that everything has shifted down one string and the character of the sound has changed. Next, retune to D (D A D F# A D) and play the same melody again:

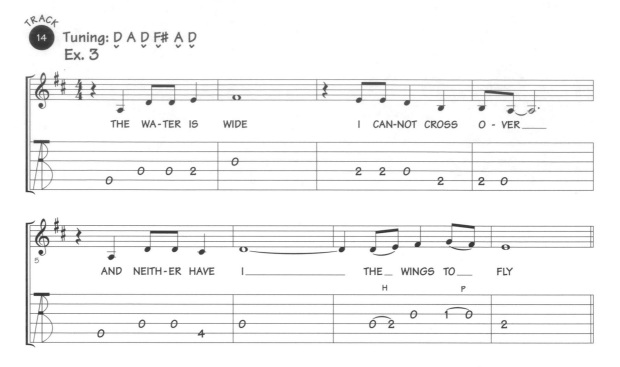

This time, the melody has shifted down another string. Now the melody is starting to feel a little low, so let's shift it up an octave:

Since the fifth and fourth strings have octave counterparts on the second and first strings, it's easy to shift the melody up to those strings. You'll also notice that in each of these tunings the bass strings have octave counterparts on the treble end.

There you have it. You can now play the same melody in three different keys without using a capo and without learning three different fingerings. If you learn something in D tuning and then start working with a singer who sings it in C, you won't have to capo up to the tenth fret and play on the short hairs, and you won't need to spend hours relearning the piece. Just retune to C tuning and shift everything over two strings.

What if we add bass notes to our arrangement of "The Water Is Wide"? When we change tunings, a note on the sixth string could end up on the . . . *seventh string?* Oops! Take a careful look and you'll see that in all three tunings, the sixth and fourth strings are tuned to the same note an octave apart. So, when you change tunings, that phantom seventh string would be tuned to the same note as the fifth string, and that's one place where you can play those missing notes.

I hope you've gained an understanding of how to transpose single-line melodies from one open tuning to another. In the next lesson, we'll see how these principles relate to chords and minor/modal tunings. In the meantime, burn that little open tunings road map into your brain until you can find your way home on a moonless night.

Finding Chords

PAUL REISLER

Tune-up: TRACK
Open D   16

Now that we've seen in the previous lesson how the three major open tunings (D, G, and C) are related to each other, let's explore how to form chords in these tunings. Since the tunings are all related to one another, you'll be able to use the chords you learn in all three tunings.

First let's look at how chords are constructed. The basic building block of Western harmony is the triad—three notes. Triads are built by starting on any note of the scale and adding two other notes of the scale. A triad on the first degree of the scale will be constructed of the 1, 3, and 5 notes on our fingerboard chart. A chord built on the second degree is made up of 2, 4, and 6. On the fourth, it's 4, 6, and 1. You get the idea.

Since guitars have six strings, you may be playing some of the notes of the chord in two places when you strum. For instance, you might have three strings sounding the bottom note, one sounding the middle note, and two sounding the top note (like when you strum the open strings of an open-D tuning: D A D F♯ A D). Variations in how these notes are arranged are called voicings. Each voicing gives the chord a slightly different hue, but they don't change the basic color.

You'll notice that in our three major open tunings, the open strings are tuned to the 1, 3, and 5 of the scale—the tonic or I chord. We can play that chord open, then barre the whole shebang at the fifth fret to get the IV chord. Barring at the seventh fret gives us the V chord, and when we barre at the 12th fret we get the I chord again. Just by using a one-finger barre we can get a I–IV–V–I progression—the three most common chords in any key.

Put your guitar in D tuning: D A D F♯ A D. With your fretboard chart in front of you, find a way of playing the chord built on the tonic. The notes are 1, 3, and 5. Here are some possibilities in D tuning. Notice that although they all sound a little different due to the voicings, they are the same chord.

Now try a few possibilities for the IV chord (using the 4, 6, and 1 of the scale):

Do the same with the V chord (using the 5, 7, and 2):

It is easy to get confused by the nomenclature for chords and scales. We use the numbers 1–7 to indicate the degrees of the scale. When we build a chord on the second, we use the 2, 4, and 6. However, when we refer to the chord, we often call the root of the chord the 1, the middle note the third, and the highest note the fifth of the chord. Yet they are still the 2, 4, and 6 of the scale.

Up until now we've been playing a bit by the numbers. It's time to talk about the way things sound. Try playing the diatonic chords (those that use only notes in the scale) built on each degree of the D scale (D, E, F♯, G, A, B, C♯):

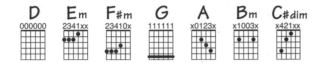

Notice that they have different qualities. Some of the chords are major chords, some are minor, and one is diminished. The major chords consist of the root of the chord, the major third (four half steps or frets above the root), and the fifth (seven half steps above the root). The minor triads are made up of the root, the minor third (three half steps above the root), and the fifth. The oddball is the diminished chord, which consists of a root, a minor third, and a diminished fifth (six half steps above the root). To generalize, we might say that the major chord has a happy quality, the minor a sad one, and the diminished an agitated quality.

All this occurs naturally due to the pattern of half steps and whole steps that make up the scale. The chords built on 1, 4, and 5 will be major, those built on 2, 3, and 6 are minor, and the chord built on 7 is diminished. It doesn't matter which key you are in; it's the same as long as you stick to the notes of the major scale.

Let's look at what happens when we transpose all of this to G tuning. Go ahead and put your guitar in G tuning (D G D G B D). Here are the diatonic chords in the key of G:

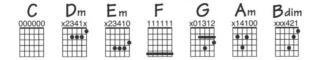

Can you see how all the formations just shifted over one string toward the treble from D tuning? It's not necessary to relearn a whole set of new chords. As with the melodies we played in the previous chapter, just shift the chords over a string and you're magically in a new key. You can play the same chords in C by retuning to C (C G C G C E), moving all the formations one more string toward the treble, and making a few adjustments for the notes that move off the neck.

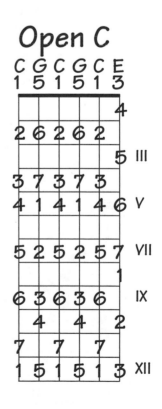

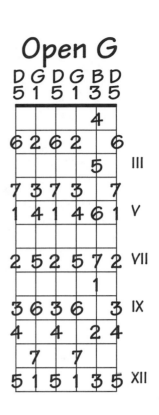

Tune-up:
Open G

You can also add notes of the scale that are not part of your basic triad. Sometimes you can get lucky just by playing an open string. Since the open strings are usually tuned to the notes of the key, you won't get a real train wreck, and often you'll discover an interesting voicing that you wouldn't have stumbled upon in standard tuning. Use your open strings. They really contribute to the sonority.

But rather than taking the hunter-gatherer approach, let's take a look at these additional notes and the chords they form. The most common addition is the seventh note above the root of the chord. If you build a seventh chord on the first degree of the scale it will contain the 1, 3, 5, and 7 notes. A seventh chord on the second degree contains the 2, 4, 6, and 1. Notice that once again the chord is built by adding alternating notes of the scale above the root note (for example, skip 2, use 3, skip 4, use 5, etc.).

Those are the chords in terms of the degrees of the scale. However, as I mentioned earlier, when we talk of chords we think in terms of the root, third, fifth, and seventh of the chord even though it may be built on any scale degree. So if we build a chord on the second, that second becomes the root of our chord. Here's another way to think of it: The 7 is one note below the root, so you can just add the note one scale tone below the root of the chord. Here are the seventh chords in D tuning. Compare them to the basic triads shown earlier.

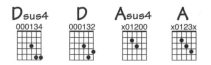

Play these chords and listen to the way they sound. Notice that they have different qualities depending on whether they are major-seventh, minor-seventh, or diminished-seventh chords and depending on the quality of the seventh. Is the seventh one half step (one fret) below the root, or a whole step below? Note that the chords built on the first and fourth are major-seventh chords (a major chord with the seventh a half step below the root), the chords built on 2, 3, and 6 are minor-seventh chords (a minor chord with the seventh a whole step below the root), the chord built on the fifth is a dominant seventh (a major chord with the seventh a whole step below the root), and the chord built on the seventh is a half-diminished-seventh chord (a diminished chord with the seventh a whole step below the root). This chord is sometimes called a minor seven flat five (m7♭5).

Let's look at other extended chords by adding other scale tones that are not part of the chord. Experiment with replacing the third of a major chord with a fourth to give you a suspended fourth (sus4) chord. The fourth wants to resolve down to the third (the old "amen" sound) as in these examples:

Now try adding the sixth above the root of the chord for a bit of a jazzy sound:

You can also add the second for a more mysterious texture. The second can replace the third (a sus2 chord) or be an addition (add9):

Dsus2 **D**add9
001300   001000

Listen closely to the way the chords sound so that you can add them to your tonal palette. One of the great things about using open tunings is that playing the open strings often adds richness and ambiguity to the chord.

Try transposing all of these chords to G tuning and then to C. Experiment with playing some songs you already know in these open tunings and see how the character has changed. Once you get the hang of it, you'll find that the music generally sounds richer than it does in standard tuning.

Dropped D, Double Dropped D, and G6

DYLAN SCHORER

Tunings that only change a string or two allow you to keep your standard-tuning points of reference handy.

Introduction and Tune-up: Dropped D

Making the leap from standard tuning to unfamiliar alternate tunings can be an intimidating experience. After spending countless hours trying to find your way around standard tuning, why subject yourself to learning a whole new set of chords and scales? In truth, however, the chords you'll use in altered tunings will often be easier than some of the finger busters you have to wrestle with in standard tuning, and they may not be that far removed from their standard-tuning counterparts. In the three tunings we're going to look at in this lesson, you'll be happy to see that a great deal of what you know about standard tuning still applies. While popular tunings like open D (D A D F# A D) seem far from standard, tunings that only change a string or two allow you to keep your standard-tuning points of reference handy. Even these slight tuning modifications will provide you with a whole new palette of sounds and textures.

One of things that prevents many guitarists from experimenting in altered tunings is the hassle of retuning. When I was learning to play I would spend a great deal of my time just trying to get in tune. If I encountered a song that was in dropped D or another tuning, I would devise all sorts of awkward fingering alternatives to avoid having to disrupt the delicate tuning balance I'd painstakingly achieved. It didn't take too long before I realized that retuning a string or two wasn't the hassle I had it made out to be—getting into a new tuning just takes a little bit of practice. When you're starting out, keep an electronic tuner nearby to check yourself.

DROPPED D

Let's start with dropped-D tuning (D A D G B E), which lowers the bass string only slightly but opens a new world of tonalities and textures. To get into dropped-D tuning, lower your sixth string from E down to D. Use your fourth string as a reference point; your sixth string should be exactly an octave lower than your fourth string. You don't need to go very far—on a steel-string guitar it typically takes less than a full turn of the tuning peg. In fact, it may be helpful to memorize roughly how far you have to turn the peg to get to D. To fine-tune, compare the pitch of the harmonic at the 12th fret of the sixth string to that of the open fourth string. You should also be aware that you'll arrive at a more stable tuning if you drop the string slightly lower than D, then raise it back up. This will prevent any string binding that can slip and drop the string out of tune.

Once you've arrived at dropped-D tuning, indulge yourself with the huge D chord you now have at your disposal. It's fingered exactly the same as a standard-tuning D chord, but you can strum all six strings now to get a nice low bass.

Keep in mind that any chords played on the top four or five strings (C, A, Am, F, Bm, etc.) in standard tuning don't need any modification at all in dropped D. Any chords that incorporate notes on the sixth string, however, will need to be modified slightly—you have to raise the note on the sixth string up two frets. For example, the standard-tuning Em chord on the left becomes the chord on the right in dropped D:

Keep in mind that any chords played on the top four or five strings (C, A, Am, F, Bm,etc.) in standard tuning don't need any modification at all in dropped D. Any chords that incorporate notes on the sixth string, however, will need to be modified slightly—you have to raise the note on the sixth string up two frets. For example, the standard-tuning Em chord on the left becomes the chord on the right in dropped D:

Some chords will need a bit more modification, however. Take a G chord, for example. The standard-tuning G is on the left. If you tried simply raising the note on the sixth string two frets you'd end up with the unplayable chord on the right:

However, we can simply omit the note on the fifth string and use the following voicing (lean your third finger lightly against the fifth string to mute it):

Dropped-D tuning gives a few chord shapes that are much simpler than their standard-tuned counterparts. For example, a power chord on the bottom strings is shown on the left in standard tuning, whereas in dropped D, we get the one-finger staple of grunge guitar on the right:

For practice try taking some songs you know in the key of D and play them using dropped-D tuning. Look for ways to incorporate the low D note and figure out how to modify chords that use notes on the bottom strings. If you can't find a comfortable fingering by just raising the bass note up two frets, try leaving out a note or two or using open strings.

Now let's look at some music in dropped D. I've shown you how to translate standard-tuning chords to dropped D, but finding new sounds that are impossible in standard tuning is the real reason for using an alternate tuning. To my ear, one of the coolest things you can do in dropped D is shift your chord voicings down to a lower register on the bottom strings to take advantage of the low bass richness. For example, instead of playing the bright, jangly-sounding open-D chord, try this warmer, darker version:

Example 1 confines all the chord voicings to the bottom strings. Try strumming it with your bare thumb instead of a pick for added warmth. Notice how the open bass notes and sparse fingering allow you the freedom to incorporate snippets of melody.

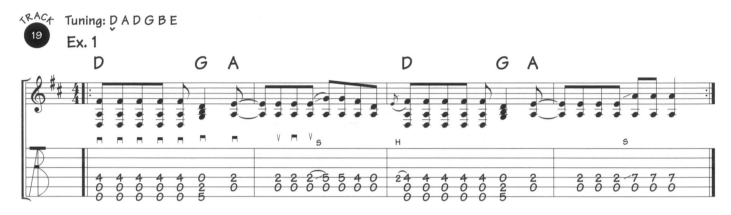

Here is a bluesy fingerpicking example in dropped D. Again, the deep, low bass gives you a strong root to play over.

Example 3 is an amped-up, pop-style groove. It has a driving rhythm with a low-string focus similar to Example 1 and some punctuated moments on the upper strings.

TRACK 21
Tuning: D A D G B E

Ex. 3

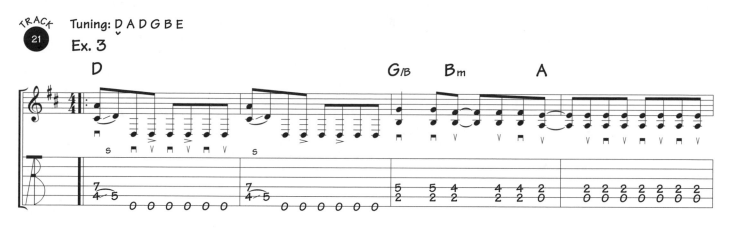

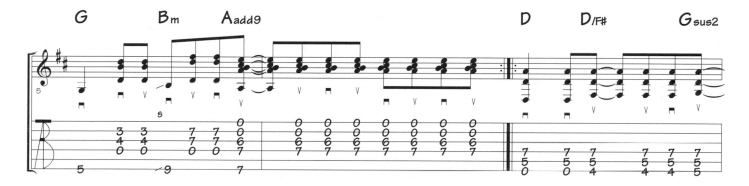

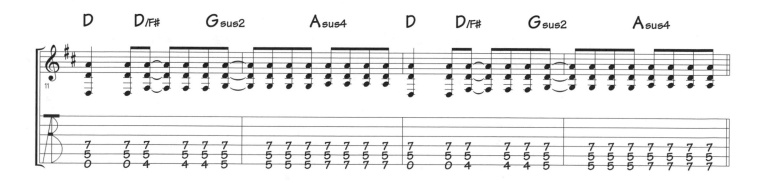

Dropped-D Chords and Scales

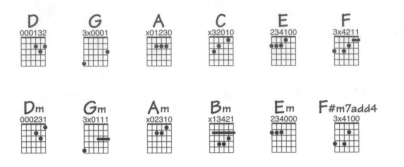

D-major scale

D-minor scale

DOUBLE DROPPED D

Tune-up:
Double Dropped D

The next tuning we'll look at is double dropped D (D A D G B D), sometimes called D-modal tuning. It's a favorite tuning of Stephen Stills and Neil Young, as well as finger-pickers like Chris Proctor.

To get into double dropped D, lower both your sixth and first strings to D. Your first string should sound the same as the third fret of your second string.

To convert chords from standard tuning into doubled dropped D, just raise the notes on the first and sixth strings up two frets. Examine the following chords and notice how they correspond to their standard-tuning counterparts:

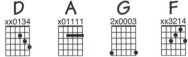

The open D on the first string offers a lot of possibilities based on the three open-D strings. For instance, try this excellent D chord:

D
000130

Countless grooves can be built around this shape with a minimum of fuss. A lot of melodic possibilities unfold by holding the chord down with your first and third fingers and using your second finger to grab a note on the third fret of any of the bottom four strings. Think Neil Young:

Example 6 builds on this idea, taking advantage of the low bass string as well as some new modal chord voicings that use the open first string. Notice the G chord in bar 4.

TRACK 25

Tuning: D A D G B D

Ex. 6

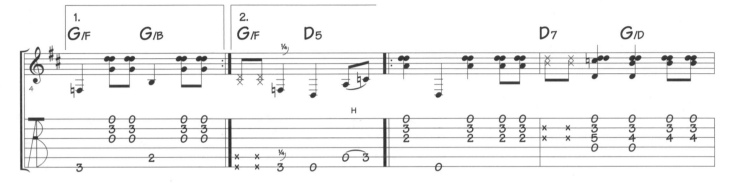

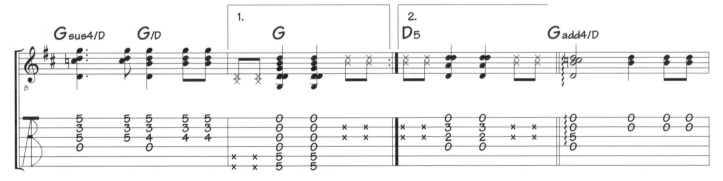

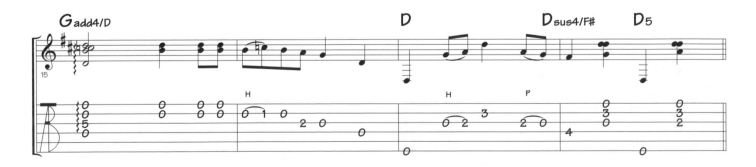

Another new sound available in this tuning is found by using the open D on the first string melodically. When you're fingerpicking, it offers some effortless, harplike effects, as illustrated in Example 7. Be sure to let each note ring into the next.

Example 8 illustrates how these effects can be incorporated into a tune.

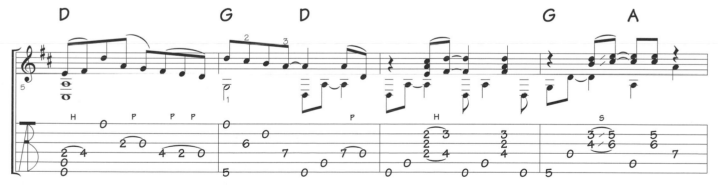

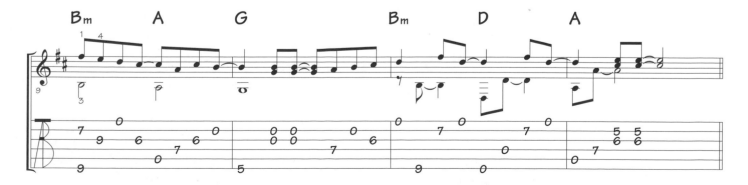

Double Dropped-D Chords and Scales

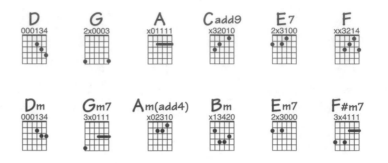

D-major scale

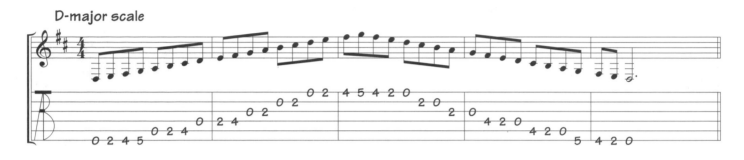

D-minor scale

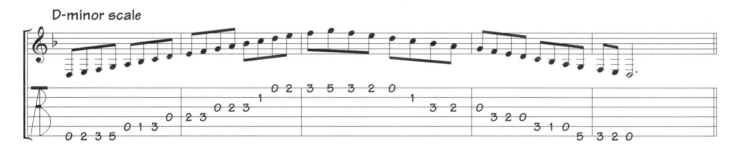

Tune-up: G6    TRACK 28

G6 TUNING

The final tuning we'll look at is D G D G B E. This is typically called G6 because if you strum all of the open strings, it produces a G6 chord. To arrive at G6 tuning, lower the sixth string down to D and drop the fifth string down one whole step to G. The fifth string should sound one octave lower than the open third string. As with the previous tunings, you only need to raise the notes on the altered strings up two frets to translate chords from standard tuning:

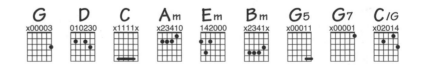

G6 tuning offers a lot of great fingerpicking opportunities. The open second, third, fourth, and fifth strings give you all the notes of a G chord. You can get a fingerpicking pattern going on those strings and move the melody up and down the neck:

G6 can also produce some powerful strumming grooves as shown in the final example, "Riverside."

To put these tunings to use, try taking songs that you already know inside and out in standard tuning and translate them into one of these tunings. Songs in the key of D work great in dropped D and double dropped D, while songs in the key of G work great in G6 tuning. However, don't be afraid to try different keys as well—songs in Em or G can also work great in dropped-D tuning. When translating songs into a new tuning, be sure to look for ways to take full advantage of the tuning by using open strings or incorporating notes into your chord voicing that weren't available in standard tuning.

G6 Chords and Scales

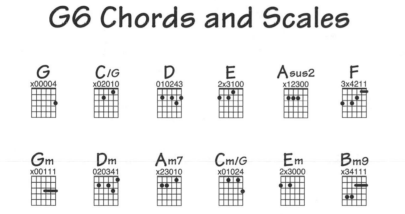

G-major scale

G-minor scale

Riverside

MUSIC BY DYLAN SCHORER

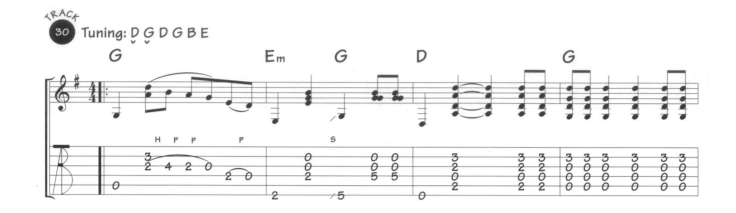

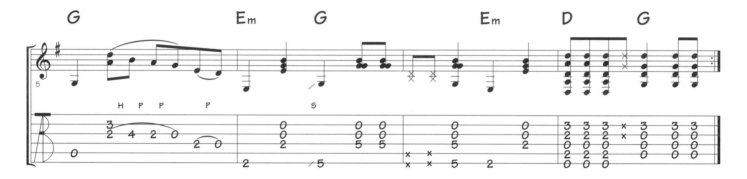

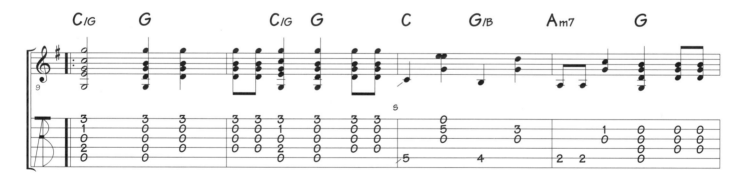

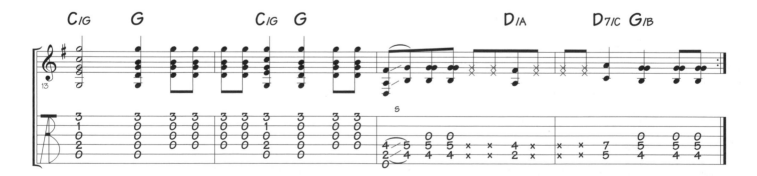

Low-C Tuning

DAVID HAMBURGER

You may have noticed that while the key of C works great for some things, such as John Hurt tunes, it doesn't offer a whole lot in terms of low end. Keys like E and A have open-string bass notes built right in, and with a key like D you can go into dropped-D tuning and have an even lower bass note to work with. But with C, the lowest C you can get is at the third fret of the A string, and you have to hold it down yourself!

Well, we're guitar players and our unwritten motto is, "There is always a mechanical solution to our musical problems." Fortunately (or unfortunately, perhaps) you won't actually need to buy any new gear to solve this problem; a little creative retuning will yield some pretty satisfying results. Roughly modeled after the dropped-D solution, the C tuning we'll check in this lesson involves tuning down just the two lowest strings. First, bring your low E string down two whole steps to C. Then bring your A string down a whole step to G. The result is C G D G B E, low to high.

Listen to what happens when you form a basic C chord. You can leave off the third fret of the fifth string because you've now got G (the fifth) on that string and a C below that on the low string:

By making a barre chord out of this shape, you can move it up to play F and G, the IV and V in the key of C:

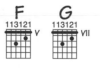

In standard tuning, barre chords are hard. They're also dry: with no open strings you don't get the ringing and resonance that makes an acoustic instrument sound and feel so good. However, retuning the two lowest strings creates more slack, making barre chords easier to hold down. And when the strings are looser, they feel and sound more resilient too. More importantly, the broad intervals between the three lowest strings give these voicings a resonance lacking in standard-tuning barre chords. Here are these voicings in a I–IV–V chord progression in C:

Modeled after dropped D, low-C tuning involves tuning down just the two lowest strings.

Introduction and Tune-up TRACK 31

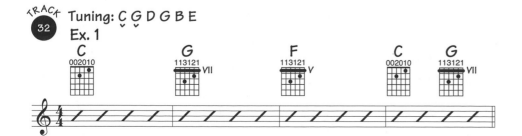

The main musical snag with using barre chords is the way everything moves in the same direction at the same time. The voice leading, as the classical cats like to call it, does not, as the jazz cognoscenti say, swing. In other words, each note of a given chord is moving the exact same distance in the exact same direction as all the other notes to get to the next chord. This is considered by some to be anywhere from slightly gauche to a profound drag.

Here are some different voicings for F and G:

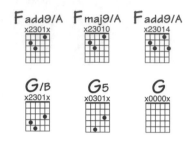

Notice that the first F voicing (Fadd9/A) and the first G voicing (G/B) use the same fingering, a whole step apart. This looks at first like the kind of thing we're trying to avoid, but these chords have open strings, unlike the barre-chord voicings, and the same open strings mean something different when you play a voicing at two different positions on the fingerboard.

Play Example 2, and listen to how different the same chord progression from Example 1 sounds now.

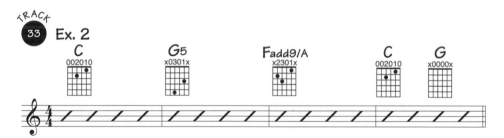

Here are some other voicings for C and G that resemble ordinary standard tuning voicings without their fretted notes from the bottom two strings:

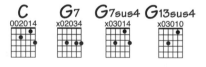

These voicings lend themselves to the idea of using a pedal point. A pedal point is a note that remains constant during a changing sequence of chords. In Example 3 the pedal point or common tone is the high G:

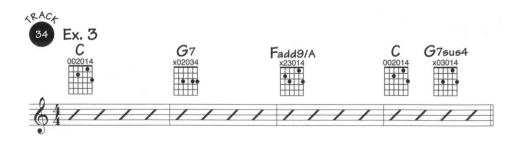

Be careful not to play the low C when playing any of these G chords. Try muting the low C with your fretting-hand thumb or practice strumming just the top five strings.

Playing diatonic sixths on the second and fourth strings will also be the same as in standard tuning:

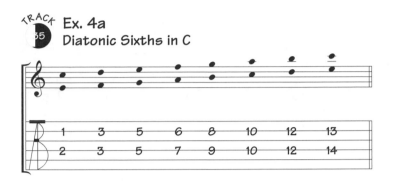

Ex. 4a
Diatonic Sixths in C

Combined with the open-C and/or open-G string, diatonic sixths provide even more ways to voice the I and V chords in C:

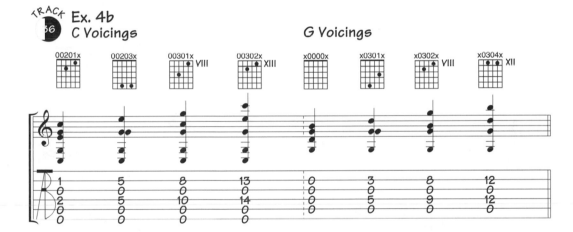

Ex. 4b
C Voicings   G Voicings

Example 5 shows another way to play our progression, making use of these additional voicings. Notice the melodic motion we create in Example 5 by being a little liberal with the use of sixths. The opening C voicing actually uses the interval of a fifth between the notes on the fourth and second strings, but the embellishment—raising the G on the second string two frets to A and then bringing it back down again—results in a sixth, at least momentarily.

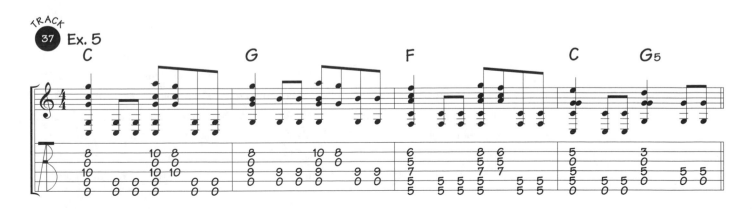

Ex. 5

You can create other embellishments by hammering onto, pulling off of, or sliding into a given chord. Here are a few ways to get in and out of the I, IV, and V chords in C:

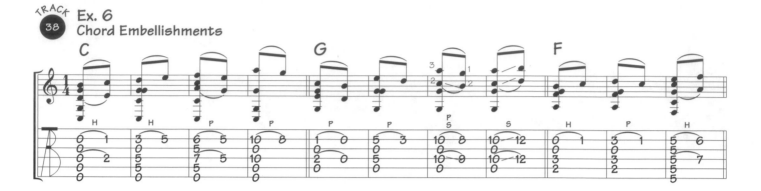

TRACK 38   **Ex. 6**
Chord Embellishments

Here's an illustration of how you might incorporate some of these moves into our progression.

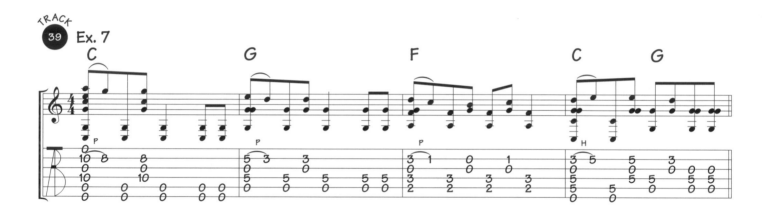

TRACK 39   **Ex. 7**

Let's look at a couple of ways to voice minor chords without barring. If you maintain an open mind about allowing things like sevenths, ninths, and 11ths into your voicings, you can end up with some pretty cool sounds for the ii, iii, and vi chords.

Dm	Em	Am
11213x	11213x	x23410

Dm11	Em9	Am7
234010	234010	x23010

To wrap things up, I've arranged "Banks of the Ohio," one of the loveliest melodies to ever clinically detail the unfolding of a needless, premeditated murder. I've made a number of diatonic chord substitutions, using chords that belong to the key as passing chords (for example, the G/B and Am7 in measures 2 and 3) or to create more color (the Dm11 in measure 14 is a particularly splashy moment). You can simply strum through the voicings as an accompaniment to the melody or actually read through the music and tab, which provide a flatpicking chord/melody arrangement of the tune itself. Good luck!

Banks of the Ohio

TRADITIONAL, ARRANGED BY DAVID HAMBURGER

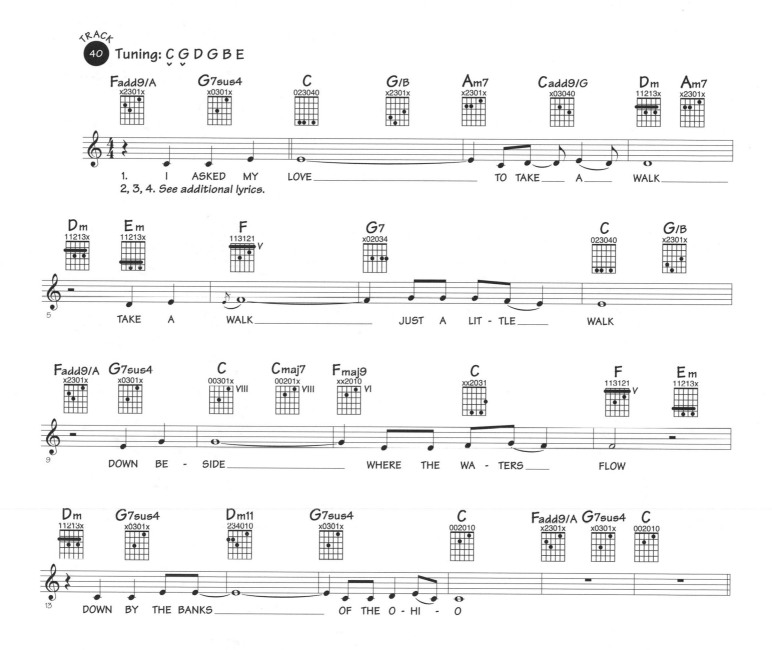

1. I ASKED MY LOVE TO TAKE A WALK
   TAKE A WALK JUST A LITTLE WALK
   DOWN BESIDE WHERE THE WATERS FLOW
   DOWN BY THE BANKS OF THE OHIO

2. AND ONLY SAY THAT YOU'LL BE MINE
   IN NO OTHER ARMS ENTWINE
   DOWN BESIDE WHERE THE WATERS FLOW
   DOWN BY THE BANKS OF THE OHIO

3. I HELD A KNIFE AGAINST HER BREAST
   AS INTO HER ARMS SHE PRESSED
   SHE CRIED, "OH WILLIE DON'T MURDER ME
   I'M NOT PREPARED FOR ETERNITY"

4. I STARTED HOME 'TWEEN 12 AND ONE
   I CRIED, "MY GOD WHAT HAVE I DONE"
   KILLED THE ONLY WOMAN I LOVED
   BECAUSE SHE WOULD NOT BE MY BRIDE

TRACK
41 **Instrumental Version**

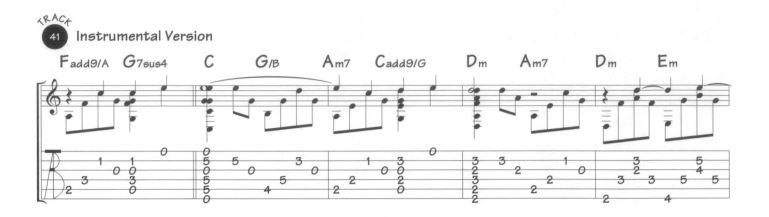

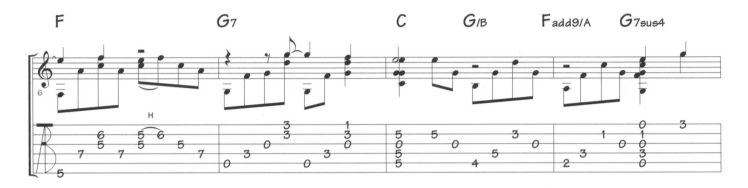

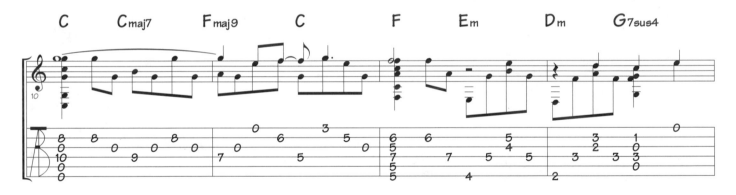

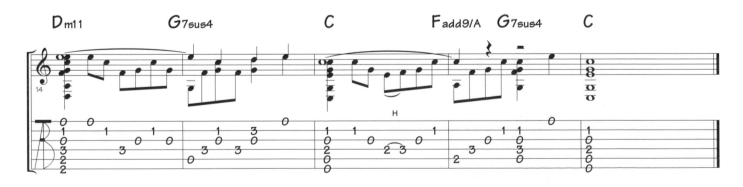

Low-C Chords and Scales

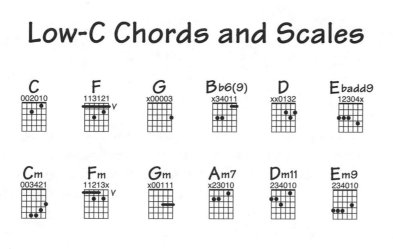

C-major scale

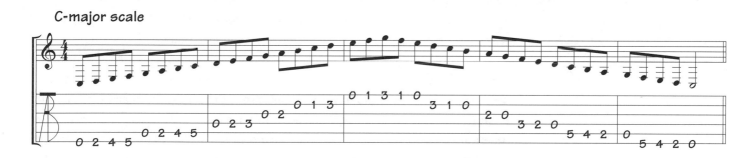

C-minor scale

Open D and Open G

STEVE JAMES

Vastopol and Spanish are two of the most common and versatile open tunings.

Introduction and Tune-up: Open D

TRACK 42

" I just been in Spanish. Put me in Vastopol," Furry Lewis said one night as he handed me his guitar. We were playing at the tiny, thronged Memphis bar called Peanuts Pub where my duties, in addition to playing second guitar for the country blues icon, included playing straight man to his acerbic humor and acting as on-stage guitar tech. Lewis' vernacular names for his preferred tunings were remarkable because they related to songs that had been popular with American guitar players more than a hundred years before.

Open chord tunings for the guitar were in common use in 16th-century Europe, where four- and five-course instruments were the norm and a universal tuning system had not yet been developed. By the end of the 1700s, as six-string guitars became available, what we now refer to as standard tuning (E A D G B E) was more prevalent, but open tunings persisted—notably in the guitar methods of the era. In this lesson we'll look at two well-known American themes of the 19th century, "Sebastopol" and "Spanish Fandango," which gave their names to two of the most common open tunings.

SEBASTOPOL

This piece employs an especially useful tuning, one that's still known and used from the *capoeira* music of Brazil to Gypsy repertoire from Russia. And it figures importantly in American roots music. Here are the notes and their scale degrees (in the key of D), from the lowest (sixth) string to the highest (first) string.

D	A	D	F♯	A	D
1	5	1	3	5	1

This tuning is composed of notes that correspond to a D-major chord triad; that's why it's commonly referred to as open D as well as Sebastopol or Vastopol. To get into Sebastopol from standard tuning, first drop the sixth (lowest) string down a whole step to D, an octave below the fourth string. Then lower the first string a whole step to D, an octave above the fourth string. Drop the second string a whole step to A, an octave above the fifth string, and finally drop the third string a half step to F♯ so that the open third string matches the fourth fret on the fourth string. On track 42 in the accompanying audio, you can hear the pitches to make sure you've tuned correctly.

Sebastopol tuning can be also achieved by using any root note on the sixth, fourth, and first strings and tuning accordingly. For example, this open-E tuning has the same note relationships, but a whole step higher:

E	B	E	G♯	B	E
1	5	1	3	5	1

The arrangement of "Sebastopol" on page 46 was published by guitar virtuoso Henry Worral in 1887 (based on an earlier version). Sebastopol, a principal seaport in Russian Transcaucasia, gained worldwide attention during the Crimean War when it fell to the French and Turks after a 349-day siege (1854–55). The entire tune, "a descriptive fantasie," occupies four pages of sheet music and is available through the International Guitar Research Institute at the University of California, Northridge. Transcribing the original to tablature was interesting since the style of methods of that era was to set the music in standard tuning with the understanding that the guitar would actually be tuned differently (hmm). The sixth, fifth, and fourth strings are to be played with the thumb; the melody is played by the fingers on the upper three strings.

Open-D Chords and Scales

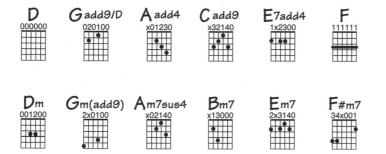

D
000000

Gadd9/D
020100

Aadd4
x01230

Cadd9
x32140

E7add4
1x2300

F
111111

Dm
001200

Gm(add9)
2x0100

Am7sus4
x02140

Bm7
x13000

Em7
2x3140

F#m7
34x001

D-major scale

D-minor scale

Sebastopol

TRADITIONAL, ARRANGED BY HENRY WORRAL

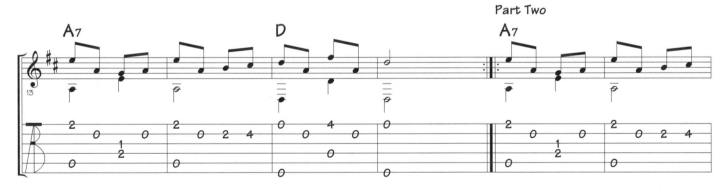

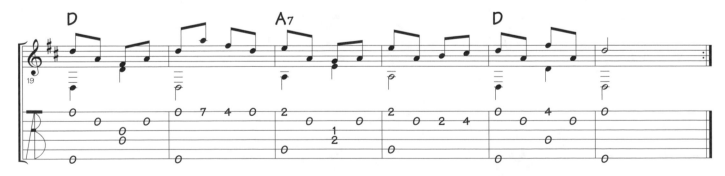

SPANISH FANDANGO

"I was agreeably entertained with seeing my landlord and landlady dance the fandango to the music of the guitar. The person who played on it struck merely a few chords in triple time. The dance itself is for two persons. . . . Every part of the body is in motion and is thrown into all postures . . . frequently very indecent ones."

—*English traveler in Spain, ca. 1772*

Derived from the influential guitar music of 18th-century Spain, this waltz was quite popular with American guitarists of the 1800s, and numerous arrangements were published. Here are the first two parts of Henry Worral's transcription, based on an 1860 version by J. and L. Peters. "Spanish Fandango" is one of the true parent pieces in American guitar music, and many recorded versions exist. (Some, like those of John Hurt and John "Seven-Foot Dilly" Dilleshaw, bear only a tangential resemblance to the one here.)

Once again, the tuning is formed from a major-chord triad—a G chord—and the same intervals can be used in different keys. Note how in this tuning the root note, G, is found on the fifth string rather than the sixth.

D	G	D	G	B	D
5	1	5	1	3	1

Here's how you get into open-G tuning, aka "Spanish," from standard tuning: Drop the sixth string down a whole step to D (an octave below the fourth string), then lower the first string a whole step to D (an octave above the fourth string). Finally, drop the fifth string a whole step to G (an octave below the third string). Check your tuning against the pitches on audio track 44.

Worral's arrangement, like the original Spanish dance, is in 6/8 time and consists of a series of arpeggios. Play strings six through three with your thumb, the second string with your index finger, and the first string with your middle finger.

Tune-up: Open G

Spanish Fandango

TRADITIONAL, ARRANGED BY HENRY WORRAL

Tuning: D G D G B D

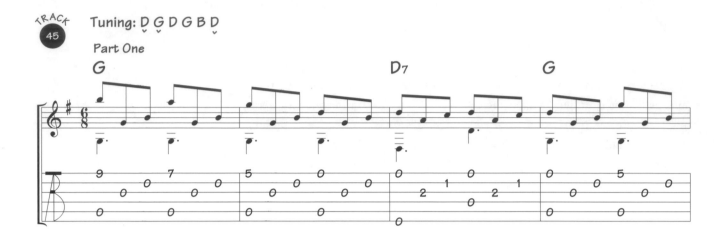

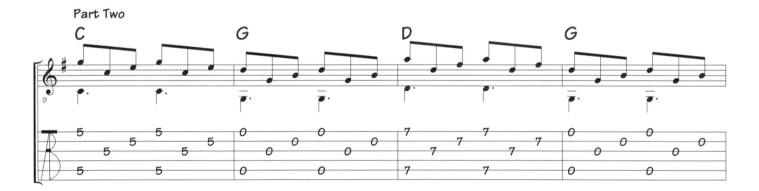

Open-G Chords and Scales

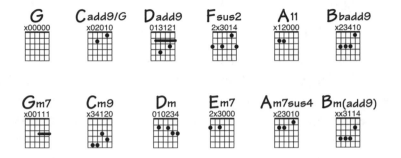

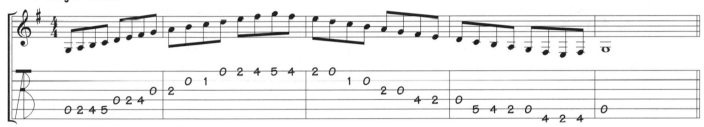

G-major scale

G-minor scale

Country Blues in Open C

DAVID HAMBURGER

Open-C tuning is a flavorful alternative to the more familiar open-D and open-G tunings.

Introduction and Tune-up

As guitar players we sometimes think of blues and country as being two completely different worlds, one thumpy and droney and shuffle-based, the other bright and sprightly and uniformly two-beat. Of course, blues and country have been cross-pollinating for a good long time, whether the results are the relaxed lilt of Mississippi John Hurt doing an old murder ballad or Merle Travis squeezing out jazzy chord licks over a poppin' two-beat feel. In this lesson we'll take a look at open-C tuning and start developing a countrified blues vocabulary that will work over an alternating-thumb bass. Open C's lower bass register and higher intervals on top make for some interesting voicing and single-note possibilities that are worth exploring, and it's a flavorful alternative to the more familiar open-D and open-G tunings.

If you're at all familiar with open D or open G, you've got some reference points already for checking out open C. The basic idea is the same: strum all the open strings and you get a big fat chord; form your IV and V chords by either barring at the fifth and seventh frets or make alternative voicings in the open position that may or may not have the root of the chord as the bottom note.

To get into open-C tuning, tune the low E string down two whole steps to C. Bring the A string down a whole step to G and the D string down a whole step to C. Leave the G string where it is, raise the B string a half step to C, and leave the high E string alone. From low to high, the tuning is: C G C G C E.

We'll stick with three basic open-position voicings for this lesson, since our emphasis is going to be on working out various licks and melodies over the I, IV, and V chords. Here are the voicings we'll be using for C, F, and G:

C
000000

F/A
x20301

G5
x02034

As you may know if you've done any single-note blues soloing with another guitar player or a band, one of the great beauties of the minor pentatonic scale is the way the same phrases seem to work over all three chords of a blues progression. Here's one fingering for an octave and a half of the C-minor pentatonic scale in open position:

TRACK 47

Tuning: C G C G C E

Ex. 1

C-minor pentatonic scale

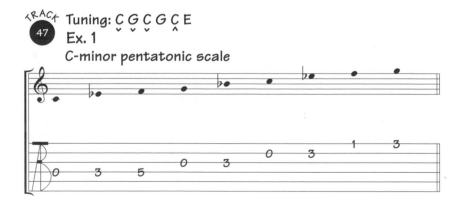

Now let's try playing a simple phrase worked out over an alternating-thumb accompaniment with a C chord, an F chord, and a G chord:

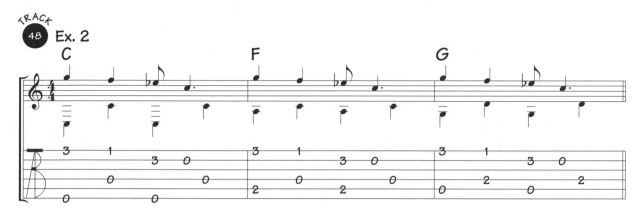

When you use the minor pentatonic scale, you need to find some way to raise the minor third toward the major third. Finessing this move with a bend of some kind is one of the characteristic sounds of the blues. The idea is to get the note about halfway up from the minor third to the major third. In other words, on a blues in C you'd want to bend the E♭ (the minor third of the pentatonic scale) up toward an E♮ without quite getting there. In Example 3, an eight-bar blues, there are two quarter-step bends, one in measure 2 and one in measure 4.

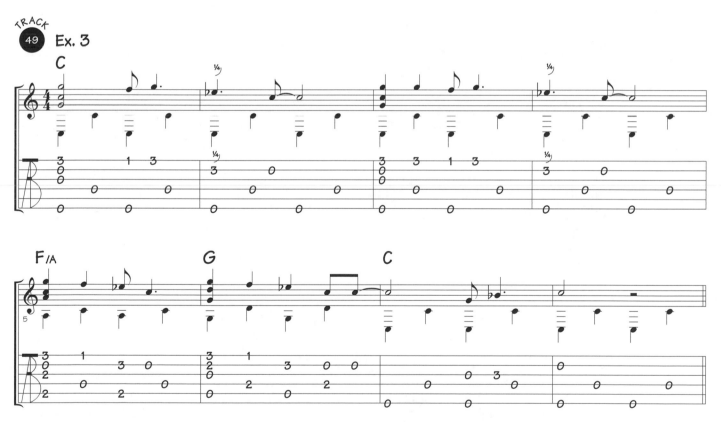

One thing that might make the open-C terrain seem more familiar is the fact that the third and second strings are the fifth and root of the key of C (G and C). This is similar to the relationship of the top two strings in standard tuning (the fifth and root of the key of E: B and E) and the top two strings in open D (the fifth and root of the key of D: A and D). So you may start to recognize some of the licks on the third and second strings in C tuning if you think of them as being transposed down one string from standard or open-D tuning.

Now let's see how the major pentatonic scale fits into the picture. Here's an octave-and-a-half fingering of the C-major pentatonic scale in open position:

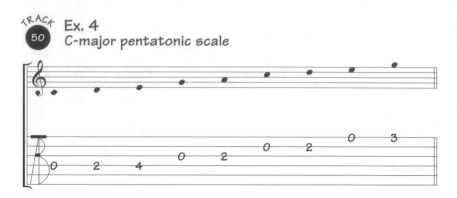

Ex. 4
TRACK 50
C-major pentatonic scale

Unlike the minor pentatonic scale, the major pentatonic scale includes the major third. It still sounds better to color the third somehow—sliding up to it from a whole step below works well. Example 5, another eight-bar progression, includes one such slide in measure 3. At the beginning of measure 1 and measure 5, the major third is played on the open high string to allow the hammer-on to the third fret.

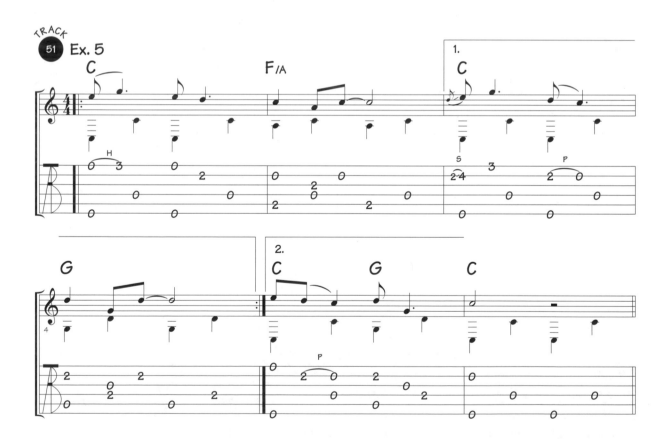

TRACK 51 **Ex. 5**

You can get a lot of ideas for single-note licks—phrases that might make good fills or soloing ideas—by experimenting with these two scales in C tuning. These two phrases show how you can take the same basic idea and work it out as either a major (Example 6a) or minor (Example 6b) pentatonic lick:

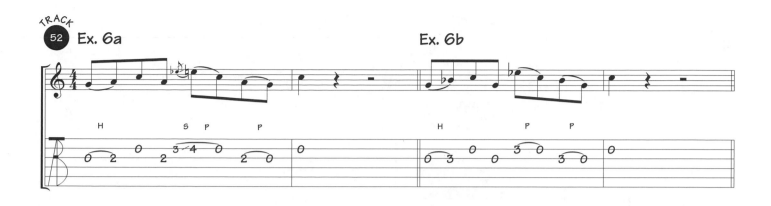

Some of the best sounds come from combining the two scales into a single phrase:

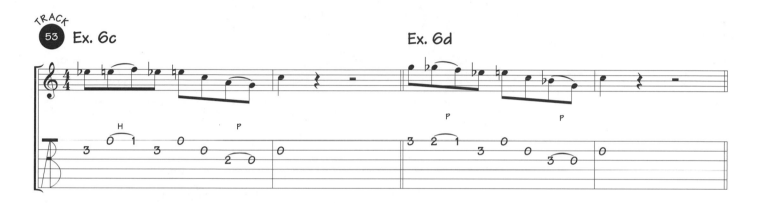

And because the fifth and fourth strings, G and C, are the same as the third and second strings an octave down, you can play things like Examples 6e, which is basically 6a an octave down, and 6f:

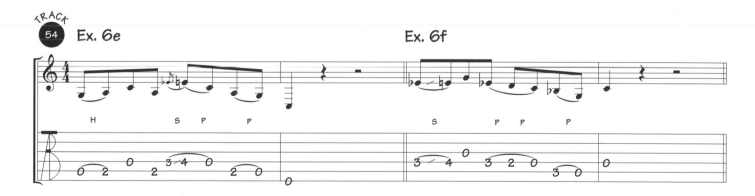

Example 7 illustrates how some of these kinds of eighth-note phrases could work in an eight-bar blues. Notice how the alternating bass drops out in measure 7, to be replaced with a single-note, stop-time lick in the bass register. This can be an effective way to break up the regularity of the alternating thumb pattern while maintaining the groove. The double-stop figure in measures 1 and 5 is particularly cool, and you could work out more sixths like that up the neck. If you do, note that all the shapes will be the same as in standard tuning, as the first and third strings are still E and G, just like in standard tuning.

Finally, I've included an arrangement of the traditional tune "I Am a Pilgrim." The melody is essentially a major pentatonic theme set over the I, IV, and V chord voicings we've been using. There's a John Hurt–type major/minor pentatonic fill in measure 7 and a big flashy four-bar cadenza at the end to round things out. Note the chromatic move at the end of measure 16 (A to A♭ to G) and the triplet in the middle of measure 17.

I Am a Pilgrim

TRADITIONAL, ARRANGED BY DAVID HAMBURGER

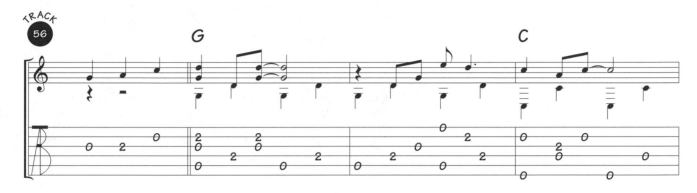

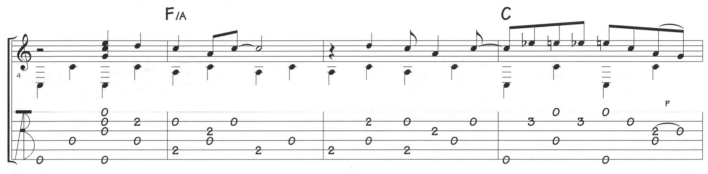

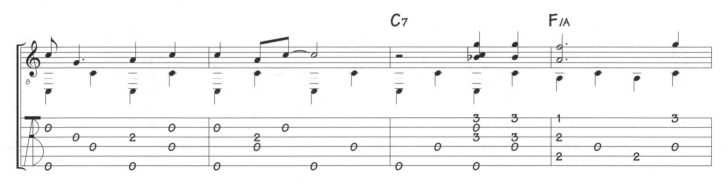

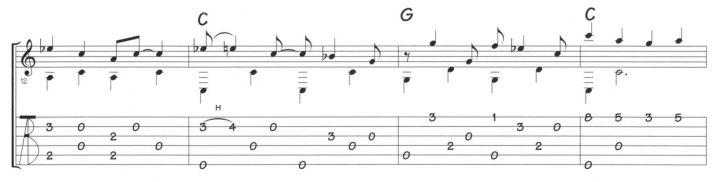

Open-C Chords and Scales

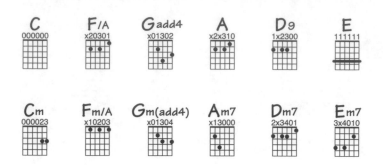

C-major scale

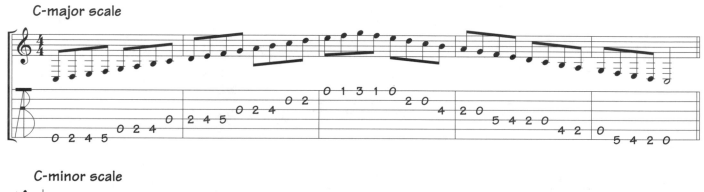

C-minor scale

The Magic of D A D G A D

AL PETTEWAY

The experience of playing a guitar in D A D G A D tuning for the first time is like magic. Simply tuning the first, second, and sixth strings down by one whole step transforms the fingerboard into a landscape of unexplored possibilities where most previously learned left-hand patterns no longer apply, yet every exploration leads to something new and interesting. The magic happens immediately upon strumming the open strings. The root/fifth relationship between the open D's and A's is comfortable and easily recognizable, while the addition of the open G string in the midst of all of this comfort creates a beautiful suspension.

By pressing down only the G string on the second fret, the suspension is resolved to create a D chord with no third. Pressing down the fifth string at the second fret creates a beautiful variation of G major with a suspended second (A) on the second string. Another simple move of the finger to the fourth string on the second fret creates a version of A7 (V) with a suspended fourth (D) on the first string and again no third. So, with only one finger, the three most commonly used chords in the key of D can be played in a new and instantly pleasing way.

A whole world of beautiful cascading scales and suspended chords will reveal themselves in different keys and positions.

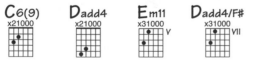

Chords and scale patterns that combine fingered notes with open strings give D A D G A D its unique character. It's easy to create chords that include sixths or suspended seconds and fourths simply by letting some open strings ring. The open first and second strings are often used the way drones are used on bagpipes. Their harmonic relationship to the chords and melodic lines will change, depending on the key, but the droning open strings can be used effectively to provide continuity and grounding in an arrangement. Playing only the root and third of any chord in the key of D (fingered on any two strings anywhere on the fingerboard) with the adjacent open strings creates rich and interesting chord variations:

Introduction and Tune-up TRACK 57

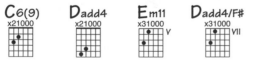

Experiment freely and listen closely. Before long, a whole world of beautiful cascading scales and suspended chords will reveal themselves in different keys and positions. D A D G A D tuning can provide some of the most creative and magical moments of any guitarist's education on the instrument. So enjoy it!

CHORD POSITIONS

The first row of chord diagrams below illustrates how a few chords translated from standard tuning might look and sound. The second and third rows show a few variations of standard chords that take advantage of the open strings. The last row shows some very simple chord shapes that can be used anywhere on the neck (in combination with the open strings) as substitutes for some of the more standard major and minor chords.

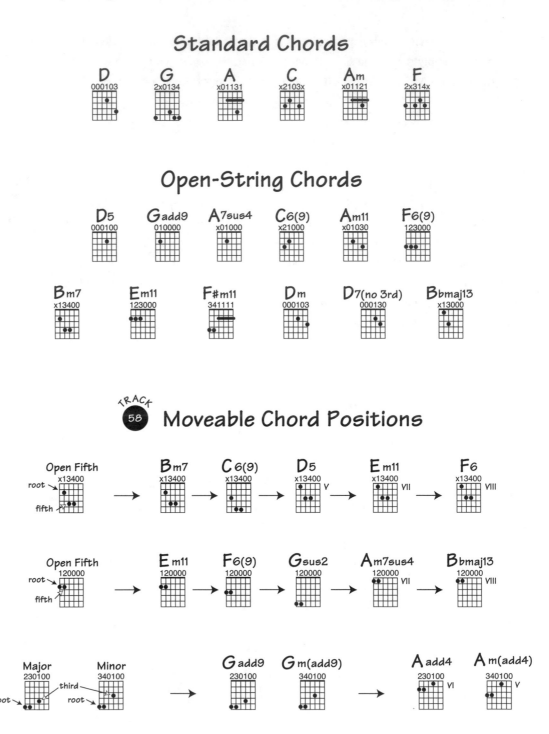

SCALES

In any tuning, it's helpful to play in left-hand positions that contain all the available scale tones of a given key or mode. The fingers of the left hand should line up on adjacent frets to allow for economy of movement. Here are a few basic left-hand scale patterns for D A D G A D. Think of these patterns as "safe zones" within these particular keys or modes.

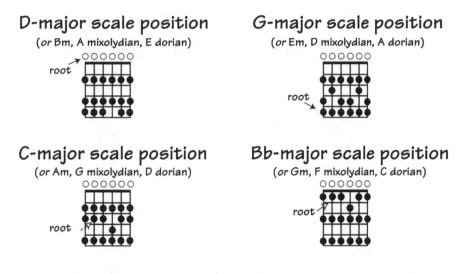

After identifying the root note of a key or mode, try playing the surrounding notes in the pattern and listening to how they relate to that root note. These patterns can also be used anywhere on the neck, with or without a capo, as long as you know the location of the root note. Some of the notes in the pattern are exactly the same as a note on an adjacent string. The choice of fingering will depend on the context in which the note is used. Some fingerings sound better or are easier to play than others, and you should experiment with each fingering.

FINGERSTYLE ARRANGING

When arranging tunes for fingerstyle guitar, it's best to start by finding a key in which the melody and bass lines fall easily under your fingers. Try two or three keys and pick the one that allows you the easiest access to the tune's entire melody. Add the appropriate bass notes in that key and finally fill in whatever chords you deem necessary. You can also make the arrangement more interesting with some tasteful use of ornamentation.

"She Moved through the Faire" is a haunting Irish ballad that lends itself well to a variety of fingerstyle guitar arrangements. The melody is all in a D-mixolydian mode, which is simply a D-major scale with a flatted 7th (C rather than C♯). I've added some simple ornamentation during the repeat (measures 18–33). Since traditional melodies are often repeated a number of times, it's important to provide listeners with some variety. A change in the accompaniment and/or ornamentation during each repetition will keep the piece fresh. This song is often sung in a rather free, conversational way. Try adding space at the end of each musical phrase the way a storyteller inserts a pause to increase the impact of a line in a story. Also, try placing a capo on the fifth fret to change the key to G and listen for the change in tonal quality.

"Morrison's Jig" is one of the most popular tunes in traditional Irish music. The melody is based in the E-dorian mode, which sounds like E minor but has a raised 6th (C♯ instead of C). E dorian also contains the same notes as D major. In my arrangement on page 61, the melody is played using a combination of fingered and open strings to create a harplike effect. I've also added a simple bass line to suggest chord changes.

She Moved through the Faire

TRADITIONAL, ARRANGED BY AL PETTEWAY

Morrison's Jig

TRADITIONAL, ARRANGED BY AL PETTEWAY

TRACK 60 Tuning: D A D G A D

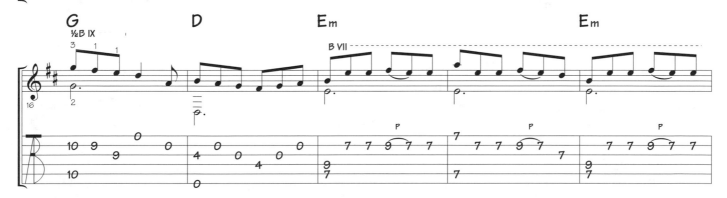

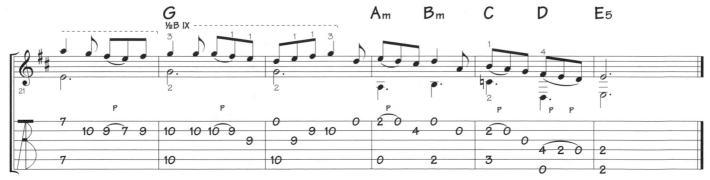

CELTIC RHYTHM

D A D G A D is an ideal tuning for rhythm accompaniment, especially in Celtic music. Simple chord shapes ring with the addition of open strings to create compelling suspensions and tonal continuity from chord to chord. Easy chord substitutions can spice up an otherwise repetitive accompaniment. In the following example, I've given you three ways to accompany "Morrison's Jig." The chord accompaniment changes with every repetition, and each of the three variations takes a few more liberties with the harmonic structure of the tune.

Discovering Your Own Tunings

GARY JOYNER

Altered tunings provide a path back to the sense of adventure we felt when we first picked up a guitar.

You have been learning to find your way around in several of the most popular altered tunings. Each offers a tantalizing landscape of possibilities to explore. At some point, though, you'll want to create your own variations and new tunings. Here are some signposts that will help you find your way across the new terrain. Remember to visualize each string as an interval in the chord implied by the open strings. The D A D F♯ A D of open-D tuning will most readily be identified as R 5 R 3 5 R. The grouping of root-fifth-root is important because it occurs in many tunings.

The convenient solitary third that occurs in each of the three basic tunings is a good place to begin further tweaking. Modality is determined by the third. If you lower it one half step you will have a minor tuning. D major (D A D F♯ A D) becomes D minor (D A D F A D or R 5 R ♭3 5 R). Lower the second string a half step in G major (D G D G B D) and you get G minor (D G D G B♭ D or 5 R 5 R ♭3 5). C major is C G C G C E; C minor is C G C G C E♭ (R 5 R 5 R ♭3), with the first string a half step lower. In each case, root-fifth-root is still there as a frame of reference.

You may want to get rid of the third entirely by changing it to a second or a fourth, thereby eliminating the major-minor identity. If you raise the third a half step to a fourth, G-major tuning becomes G suspended fourth, or D G D G C D. The same process applied to D-major tuning makes it the popular D suspended fourth, better known as D A D G A D. C major becomes C G C G C F. Root-fifth-root is still at your beck and call.

Lowering the third a whole step makes it a second. C major becomes C suspended second—C G C G C D, a favorite of Martin Simpson. "I'll often put a fourth in there on the third string as well, making C G C F C D," he says. "Think about that in terms of intervals and what you have is root-fifth-root-fourth in the bass, which is the same as D A D G A D. But instead of having that fifth-root on top, you have root-second. I regard most of these tunings as being very closely related."

There are two immediate benefits in these realizations. 1) The tunings are not mutually exclusive. The things you learn about one can be applied to the others. 2) Your choice of tunings needn't be random. Do you want the familiar string series to be grouped on strings one to four, two to five, or three to six? Your choice of tunings is now based on a musical decision.

The three seminal tunings (open D, open G, open C) are also commonly used one step higher. Try it if you use light strings and think your guitar is up to the added strain. (I prefer to capo at the second fret to get the same results, but I do lose some available string length in the process.) You already have a formidable number of tunings at your disposal. And you haven't even started to tweak them with your own ideas. Do you see why tunings are exciting? And do you see how a bit of thoughtful observation adds to the fun?

I have been experimenting with a scalar approach to tunings. Using the intervals of the Japanese hirajoshi scale, 1 2 ♭3 5 ♭6, I constructed C G D♭ F A♭ D♭ with the F as the root. Other root possibilities become apparent with experimentation. Such a tuning, being melodic rather than harmonic in design, is especially useful for fingerstyle playing.

FINDING YOUR OWN TUNINGS

Guitarists have different techniques for arriving at a tuning. Flatpicker Beppe Gambetta's methods are utilitarian, focusing on the practical problems of each tune. Sometimes this means simply retuning one or two strings in order to mimic the phrases and ringing of Scruggs-style bluegrass banjo rolls. "My discoveries of tunings are generally related to working a song," says Gambetta. "In my song 'Highway 18' I wanted to reproduce banjo rolls in the low strings. The only way to do this was to raise the sixth string to F#. The banjo sound worked exactly as I wished and I found new configurations of chords. On 'Slow Creek' I dropped the fifth string to G and raised the sixth string to F. It worked perfectly because the tune is based on G and F chords. The two main chords have ringing open-string roots."

On Alex de Grassi's album *The Water Garden* (Tropo), the title piece is played in C G D G A D, which is D A D G A D with strings five and six lowered an additional whole step. He likes the tuning for its warm cellolike qualities and for the pianistic jazz voicings that are possible. "I get great jazz piano voicings with C G D G A D tuning," says de Grassi. "A typical jazz piano voicing is a minor-ninth voicing: ♭7-9-♭3-5. The ninth and the minor third are a half tone away, and in standard tuning you need to play them on adjacent strings unless you play it way up the neck and find the one minor-ninth chord you can play using an open string. In this tuning you can get this voicing more easily." The tuning D A D F G C, he says, has similar attractions. "It's a quality of sound, a sonority, that is perhaps unusual for the guitar. If you tried to arrange the same melody in standard tuning, it wouldn't have the same quality."

Pop musician Duncan Sheik, who burst on the scene with his self-titled debut and the song "Barely Breathing," offers a few of his favorite discoveries. "A tuning I like is E B E F# B E (R 5 R 9 5 R), an E9 thing with no third," he says. "You can play it major or minor." His second album, *Humming* (Atlantic), has a hidden track at the end, "Foreshadowing," which uses an open B-major tuning—B F# B D# F# B. Sheik uses an actual bass guitar string for that low B. "With open tunings," he says, "each time I move to another chord I experiment. I often think I know where I'm headed, but I end up in some other place and I'm much happier to be in that place."

David Crosby, the godfather of altered tunings in pop and rock music, used E B D G A D to write the classic "Guinnevere." His other tunings have a consistent oddity. They all have a unison pair in the middle—the third and fourth strings are both tuned to D. This gives him an oudlike sound. The remaining strings will vary. "My favorite tuning right now is one I used for 'Rusty and Blue' on *CPR* [Samson Music], the album with Jeff Pevar and James Raymond," says Crosby. "It's got that pair in the middle, but it's all fifths: C G D D A E. That sounds like it would be very modal. But if you play with a diminished chord shape on the middle four strings, you get a dense, lovely, crazed chord. Then if you add the bottom string in relation to it—you'll see if you try it. You get the most amazing chord on the second fret, on the fourth and seventh. Man, it's a crème-deluxe tuning."

> "I get great jazz piano voicings with C G D G A D tuning. If you tried to arrange the same melody in standard tuning, it wouldn't have the same quality."
>
> —Alex de Grassi

"The real beauty of
alternate tunings is that
things are given to you
as gifts that you never
would have come up with
consciously on your own."

—Duncan Sheik

Asked about the process he uses to discover new tunings, Crosby says, "You can dignify it with words like that, but what I do is noodle around. If you just sit there and love on a guitar, it will speak to you. If you are a tuning freak like I am, you just fool around. Take a tuning you've had for years and tweak one string one whole tone and all of a sudden it's a different world. It's endless what you can do. You can show a tuning you've been playing for ten years to a friend and immediately he'll come up with three fingerings you didn't think of. It's just so deep."

FINDING THE CHORDS

When you've found an appealing tuning, you need to seek out some chords. David Wilcox finds that sometimes "wonderful surprises happen. You pick the guitar up off the couch and start playing chord patterns from one tuning, but the guitar's in another tuning. Often it sounds horrible. But there are moments when you say, 'Wait a second, there's something cool there.'"

Some artists actually have a fairly small vocabulary of fingerings that they use in every tuning. Joni Mitchell, for instance, uses a few fingerings up and down the neck in many different tunings, generating many different chords depending on the tuning. Here are the chords, for instance, that one of her fingerings creates in "Just Like This Train" from *Court and Spark*.

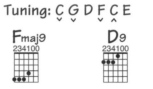

There are resources out there to help you locate chords. Mark Hanson's *Alternate Tunings Picture Chords* (Accent on Music) is a fine reference book. And five-string banjo books offer a gold mine of chord and picking ideas. Remember that banjo tunings and guitar tunings are closely related. The best use you can make of a chord book is as an analytic tool. As you study chord books, keep root-fifth-root in mind and look also for consistencies that carry over from one tuning to another.

A little music theory will serve you well. Read the "Finding Chords" lesson in this book for some theoretical grounding. If you know that adding the flatted seventh of the root to a chord will make it a dominant seventh chord, you have a valuable bit of information. The flatted seventh note can be found two frets below any root. Trace this idea in C-major tuning (C G C G C E). The G-major chord, being the V chord of the key, can be fretted with one finger across the seventh fret:

$$G$$
111111
VII

As stated earlier, the interval relationship across the neck in C tuning is R 5 R 5 R 3. Make the second-string root a flat seventh by lowering that string to the fifth fret. The open fifth string is a G. Use it as a nice low root.

You get the idea. Use your ears and your mind.

Composing in alternate tunings is a similar matter of exploration. Guitar composers tend to improvise their way to a musical idea they want to save and build upon. When you explore the ideas in this book, you will find yourself composing as if by magic. All the usual guides to composition apply—statement and response, the need for variety, a balance of surprise and predictability, melodies that can be sung, etc. The guitar will give you ideas. Try finding melodies in a key other than the tuning you're in, for instance the key of C in G tuning. In this case, you will see the D G D G B D of G tuning as 2 5 2 5 7 5 in the key of C. Start by locating the root notes (in this case, the various C notes) on the fingerboard. Duncan Sheik says, "The real beauty of alternate tunings is that things are given to you as gifts that you never would have come up with consciously on your own."

TRAPS AND INSPIRATIONS

Are there any drawbacks lurking in our fascination with peg twirling? Of course there are. You must think carefully in order to get beyond what legendary fingerstylist Pierre Bensusan, who plays almost exclusively in D A D G A D tuning, calls "the flattering sound that shines right away." He warns, "It's true that your guitar gives you ideas, feeds you. But you also have to feed your guitar from somewhere else. You have to look inside of you, not outside. Maybe it's the wrong debate to focus on alternate tunings, to focus on this tuning or that tuning. A lot of people playing in alternate tunings are stopping at the moment where they should in fact start. If you really want to master your instrument, get into a tuning in the same way that you would enter into standard tuning.

"The musical process is nonstop," Bensusan continues. "And you don't need to be only with your guitar when you are inspired. You can think, read, work with rhythms, and listen to music. Try to hear every voice of a composition, every sound played by one instrument."

At their best, altered tunings provide a path back to the sense of adventure and discovery that we felt when we first picked up a guitar. When we go to a new tuning, we enter a fresh set of limitations engendering a new level of creativity. Have fun as you take tunings beyond the limits. Martin Simpson puts it this way: "Many people never get beyond the dictation of the tuning. People who should know better say open tunings are a trap. They're only a trap if you don't explore them. Open tunings by definition will give you some limitations. Limitation is really a good thing. If you explore, you'll get a huge amount out of it."

"Take a tuning you've had for years and tweak one string one whole tone and all of a sudden it's a different world. It's endless what you can do."

—David Crosby

Arranging Bach in an Alternate Tuning

DYLAN SCHORER

Arranging an unchangeable melody begins by wrapping a tuning around the tune.

Introduction and Tune-up

'*ve always loved classical music and especially classical guitar. While I'm not a true aficionado, I've always enjoyed playing certain classical pieces. As a folkie fingerpicker, however, I always felt a little impure playing them on my steel-string with my plastic thumbpick securely in place. I loved playing them for myself, but I was much too self-conscious to perform them for others, especially after hearing countless classical guitarists perform them with a musical sensitivity and ear for the repertoire I've never attained.

Still, plinking out these classical melodies on my phosphor-bronze strings continued to be a guilty pleasure of mine. I eventually became tired of my hack renditions and began looking for ways to bring a new voice to these pieces and make them my own. Rather than approaching them with a strict attention to tradition, I decided to apply the same approach I'd been using with Celtic and American folk melodies for years and add some richness and depth by arranging them in alternate tunings. I thought that trying to find a tuning that gave the melody the most resonance and tunefulness would be perfect for the classical music I'd been working on.

One of the pieces I had been playing was the Prelude from J.S. Bach's Cello Suite No. 1, in G major (BWV 1007). Classical guitarists typically play this piece in D major, with the opening phrase wrapped around a first-position D chord:

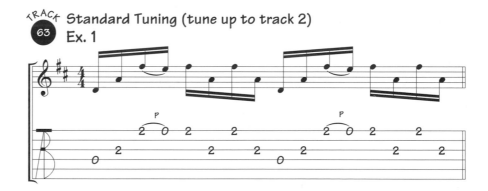

Standard Tuning (tune up to track 2)
Ex. 1

parison with the rich, resonant versions I'd heard by classical guitar masters.

Whereas composing in alternate tunings often begins with hunting and experimenting, arranging an unchangeable melody begins by wrapping a tuning around the tune, so to speak. I decided to find a tuning that would allow me to play the opening phrase with all the notes on separate strings, so the melody notes could overlap and ring into each other. This is an approach I use when arranging Irish music, and since I had recently heard an excerpt of the Bach Cello Suite performed on harp, the sound of the melody notes overlapping and flowing was fresh in my mind.

I began by experimenting with the piece in familiar tunings. I started with D A D G A D and played the piece in D as I had originally learned it, but it didn't offer the number of open strings I wanted for added resonance. I figured that since classical guitarists had transposed the piece when they originally transcribed it for guitar, I should feel free to transpose it as well. To aid in these transpositions, I put the first part of the melody into my music notation program, Finale. This allowed me to transpose the piece quickly with only a few keystrokes.

I moved to a tuning I use frequently for Irish music because of its harplike quality: C G D G C D. I tried the melody first in G and then in C in the same tuning. After playing the piece in C, it took about five seconds to realize that I should drop the fourth string down to C to get a convenient root. Thus, I arrived at the tuning C G C G C D. After playing through the first phrase, I saw that this tuning was giving me everything I wanted (see Example 2), for the first few bars anyway—I'd need to get a little further into the piece before I could commit to it.

Often when I'm arranging a new piece, I'll find a tuning where the melody falls beautifully onto the fingerboard until I reach a phrase three-quarters of the way through that is impossible to fit into the tuning in a musical way. Sometimes that means changing the tuning slightly, and making compromises with the earlier portions of the melody, or abandoning the tuning altogether and starting over. Occasionally, a portion of the melody will flow out of a tuning so musically that I just need to work a little harder to play a phrase that refuses to lie so nicely. Other times, compromises need to be made. For instance, you might have to give up an open string that added to the texture of the first phrase to avoid struggling too hard on the second phrase. Above all, musicality and consistency need to prevail. If the rhythm and texture falls flat on a certain phrase while the rest of the piece flows beautifully, you might need to look for compromises.

When I continued playing through the Cello Suite, everything fell into place until I reached bar 9. Fretting the necessary low D note on the second fret of the sixth string restricted me to playing the melody within the first five frets, which prevented me from continuing with the flowing melody I wanted. A quick scan through the piece showed me that I was never going to need the low, open-string C on the bottom, while a low D would be used several times. So, I raised the sixth string up to D to arrive at the tuning D G C G C D, which is the final tuning shown in my complete arrangement. Sure, I encountered a few phrases such as those in bars 11 and 13 that didn't lie on the fingerboard quite as comfortably as the rest, but I felt happy that the piece as a whole fit into the tuning with the right combination of resonant, overlapping melody notes and single-string movement for contrast.

I hope you enjoy playing this arrangement, but more importantly, I hope you'll use these ideas to try to give a new voice to the melodies you arrange.

Prelude from Cello Suite No. 1 (BWV 1007)

MUSIC BY J.S. BACH, ARRANGED BY DYLAN SCHORER

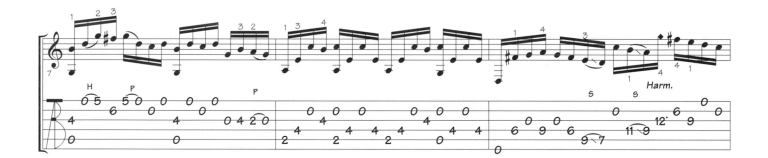

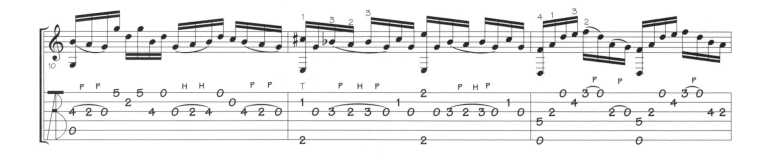

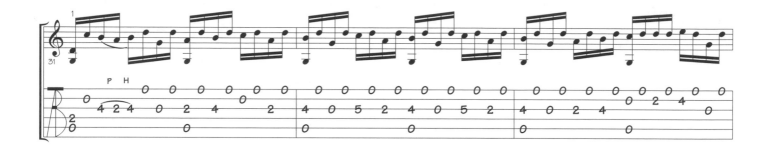

A tempo

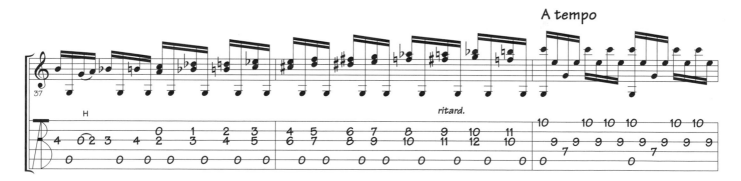

New Approaches to Folk Melodies

SCOTT NYGAARD

I have to admit to being a bit of an alternate-tuning curmudgeon. I rarely deviate from standard tuning and dropped-D, which I tend to think of as standard tuning with a cold. This is primarily for practical reasons, the main two being an innate laziness (I hate taking more than one guitar to a gig) and the fact that as a frequent side musician I have to be ready to launch into whatever song the bandleader wants to play at the drop of a capo. I also spend a lot of time improvising, and improvisers need to be able to find the notes they want intuitively without having to think too hard about where they might be. So for the most part I stick with my favored Em11 tuning: E A D G B E.

I have, however, stumbled on a couple of tunings out of necessity. One involves simply tuning my low E string up to an F to play songs in the key of C that have a lot of Am and F chords. The only problem with this tuning is when I proceed to the next song without remembering to lower my sixth string to E, slamming into what I had hoped would be a nice fat G chord only to inflict a G/G♯ chord on an unsuspecting audience. Oops!

The subject of this lesson, however, is a tuning that I came up with to facilitate playing one particular tune: Bill Monroe's "Methodist Preacher." This lively fiddle tune is traditionally played in the key of G and begins with a long held B note on the high E string. Herein lies the problem. Hanging on that long, thin, wimpy note was not a very punchy beginning to what should be a rip-snorting hoedown. I like playing certain kinds of G songs out of E position capoed up three frets. So I tried this and found that I could get a nice rolling cross-picked beginning using the top three strings in the following position:

Introduction and Tune-up TRACK 67

Standard Tuning (tune up to track 2)
Capo III
Ex. 1

E

The problem was that I kept creating an unwanted dissonance by accidentally brushing the open third and fourth strings. "Methodist Preacher" is an unambiguous major-key tune with no bluesy or modal undertones, and those open flatted thirds and flatted sevenths were downright sinful. Since I usually use medium-gauge strings, I'm reluctant to raise the pitch of strings, and since I tend to be ignorant of alternate-tuning conventions, I didn't think to tune my fourth string all the way down to B or my third string down to E, so I tried tuning the offending strings down by just a half step to the next available note in the E-major scale. I tuned the D down to a C♯ and the G down to an F♯, creating what I think of as an E6/9 tuning: E A C♯ F♯ B E. This gives you the standard-tuning open bass notes in E (E and A) as well as those nice ringing fifths on top. The middle strings give you the sixth (C♯) and second (F♯) of E. The opening phrase of "Methodist Preacher" worked well (see Example 2) and the rest of the melody immediately fell under my fingers, even eliminating some of the long stretches I was forced to make in standard tuning.

When I started trying to find chords in this tuning, I found what alternate-tuning junkies have known for years—that I could get some great lush chords and ringing strings using just a couple of fingers. Doh! I particularly liked the way the E chord in first position sounded when I hammered from the second to the third of the chord, and I could get some rockin' grooves using this idea:

* Palm Mute

I soon began trying out various melodies that emphasized the second to third, one of which, "Rovin' on a Winter's Night," a traditional song that comes from the repertoire of the Watson family, seemed perfectly suited to my newfound tuning. I decided to take the alternate-tuning plunge and even add a lush voicing or two to this old beauty (see measures 4–5 and 11–12).

Play "Rovin'" at a slow tempo, or even rubato, to emphasize the wistful quality of the lyrics:

A rovin' on a winter's night
Drinkin' good old wine
Thinkin' about that pretty little girl
Who broke that heart of mine

The simple chord shapes are also easy to finger when it comes time to sing or back up a singer.

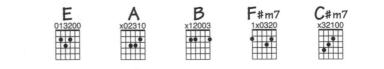

Rovin' on a Winter's Night

TRADITIONAL, ARRANGED BY SCOTT NYGAARD

TRACK 71 Tuning: E A C# F# B E
Capo III

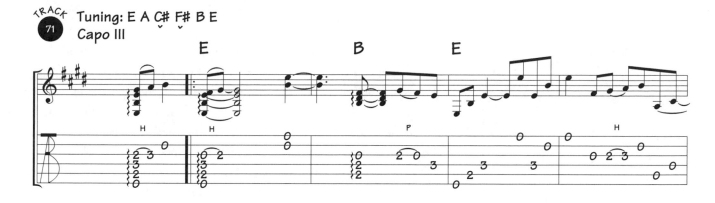

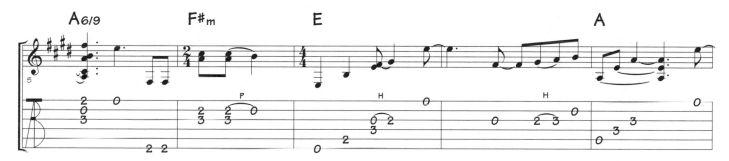

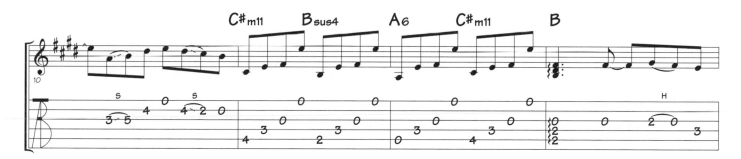

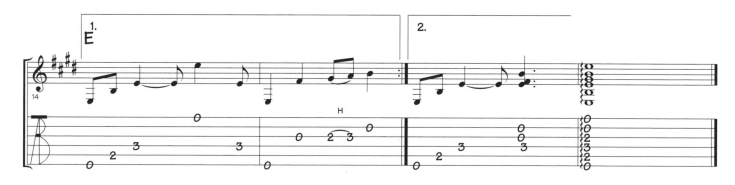

Frailing in Alternate Tunings

STEVE BAUGHMAN

A cheese tuning is any tuning in which the fourth and fifth strings are tuned in unison.

Introduction and Tune-up

TRACK 72

The joyful bounce of clawhammer banjo thrilled me the first time I heard it. Such a happy groove, so many notes, and all with such a simple little right-hand pattern. Until recently, frailing always struck me as the exclusive province of old-time banjo players. Lately, however, I have found a way to reproduce that old ricky-tick sound on the guitar, inspired by a valuable tip from Jody Stecher.

Frailing works fine in standard tuning, but the modal flavor of old-time music is best captured with open tunings. To play the traditional tune "Robert's Serenade," which I learned from a great album by Bruce Molsky and Big Hoedown, I employ what I like to call a *cheese tuning,* a term I picked up on an Internet discussion about my tune "Marche de la Fromage Grande." The term refers to any tuning in which the fourth and fifth strings are tuned in unison. This particular tuning is a B cheese, from lowest to highest E B B E A B, which I stumbled upon through random experimentation. It is fast becoming my favorite frailing tuning. The top three strings are tuned to intervals that are often used by banjo players on their first, second, and third strings. The B unisons create a bit of a drone and provide a nice modal flavor, while the sixth string provides the root.

The basic frailing pattern requires a minor adjustment of the ingrained thumb-on-the-downbeat picking style. Frailing employs the drop thumb of old-time banjo players, in which the thumb comes down on the upbeat and the fingers play the melody notes. The banjo picker's thumb usually strikes the highest pitched string (the shorter fifth string), but when frailing the guitar the thumb picks the lowest string. The basic pattern is as follows (see Example 1): Play beats 1 and 3 by picking upward with your index finger as you normally would. Play beats 2 and 4 by striking downward with the back of the nail on your middle finger, followed by your thumb on the *and* of beats 2 and 4.

TRACK 73 Tuning: E B B E A B
Ex. 1
Basic frailing pattern

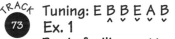

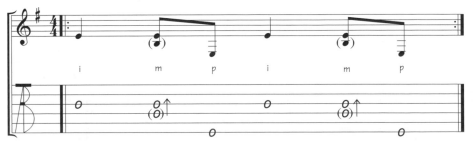

This pattern can change your sound forever. You should master it before proceeding on to "Robert's Serenade" for two reasons. First, internalizing the pattern will help purge you of any ingrained Travis-picking habits. Second, this arrangement of "Robert's Serenade" does not strictly follow the basic pattern. It often varies the pattern by omitting a note, usually the thumb. It is important that you be firmly grounded in the basic pattern before moving on to any variations.

Many tunes can be played without departing from the basic right-hand pattern. Old-time fiddlers and banjo pickers often use the same right-hand pattern over and over. This is part of the distinctive sound of old-time music, and departures from the established pattern tend to disrupt the flow. When frailing the guitar, the goal is to mimic the fiddler's bowing hand or the clawhammer of the banjo player to get that same mesmerizing groove. The right hand should be on autopilot, only to be disturbed when absolutely necessary.

But most fiddle tunes have a lot more notes than the basic frailing pattern can accommodate. What do you do if the note you want falls outside the rhythmic structure? Most often a left-hand filler slap can deal with any missing notes. This little device is a close relative of the hammer-on and is a wonderful tool for keeping a groove or a melody going without disrupting your right-hand repetitions.

The generic hammer-on is played by a left-hand finger attacking a string that has just been plucked with the right hand. The filler slap, by contrast, lands on a string that has not been plucked. Both devices give you more notes than your right hand is playing, but the filler slap provides more flexibility.

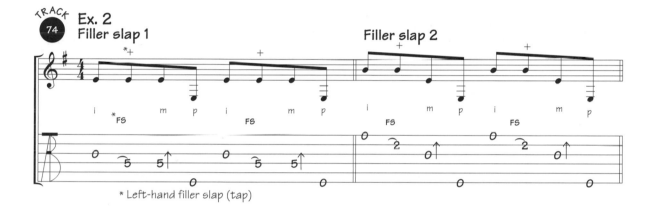

* Left-hand filler slap (tap)

I use the filler slap in "Robert's Serenade" on notes that are more aptly viewed as groove notes than melody notes. The melody notes all happen to fall within the basic frailing pattern. In other tunes this may not be the case. Adding the filler slap to your repertoire will enable you to squeeze in almost any melody note, whether it fits within your right-hand pattern or not.

Frailing, once you have it down, is fun and easy. It is also likely to carry your guitar playing to many unexplored places.

Robert's Serenade

TRADITIONAL, ARRANGED BY STEVE BAUGHMAN

** Left-hand filler slap (tap)

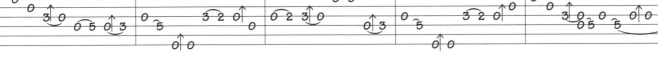

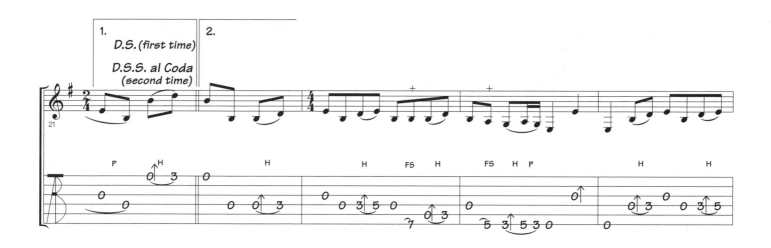

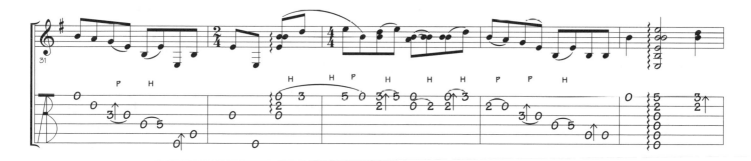

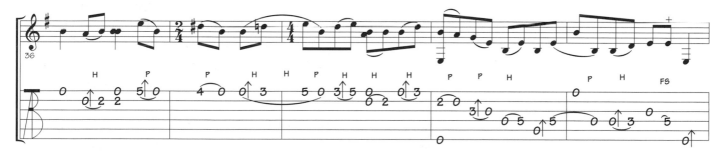

D.S.S. al D.S.S.

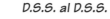

⊕ Coda

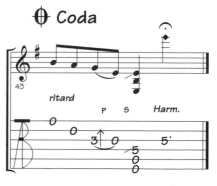

Strings, Setup, and Gizmos for Alternate Tunings

TEJA GERKEN

The perfect setup for standard tuning doesn't always work when the strings go slack.

As you get into twisting your guitar pegs, you'll discover that the perfect setup for playing in standard tuning doesn't always work when the strings go slack. If you tune down to open C, for example, that great low-action setup with light-gauge strings will probably cause your bass strings to flop around and buzz. To fix this problem, you might raise the action of your bass strings slightly and use heavier fifth and sixth strings. But then, when you tune back up to standard, they're going to feel stiff. If you want to use the same instrument to play in standard and a variety of alternate tunings, your setup will have to reflect a compromise that suits the potentially wide range of string tensions. The right compromise is a matter of personal preference, and finding it will require some experimentation.

I got a lesson in setting up for alternate tunings when I took my main steel-string, a Taylor 712C, to San Francisco Bay Area guitar tech Larry Cragg. After I told him about my needs, he set the guitar's action just a little higher than what I'd ideally keep it at for standard tuning. He made me a new saddle whose radius is slightly larger than that of my fingerboard, resulting in a slightly higher action on the bass and treble strings than on the center strings, keeping them from buzzing when they're tuned down. Cragg also made sure that my nut was cut perfectly for the string gauges I use, so that the strings don't get caught in the slots when I retune. He also smoothed out the holes in my Grover tuning pegs with a file and some very fine sandpaper so I'll be less likely to break strings when retuning.

Another thing to consider if you'll be leaving standard tuning a lot is investing in alternate tuning–friendly strings. Several companies offer sets that combine light-gauge top strings with medium-gauge bottoms. D'Addario's EJ19 Bluegrass set, for instance, goes from a .012 first string to a .056 bass string. It's perfect for tunings that drop the bass pitches and keep the trebles close to standard, such as dropped-D (D A D G B E) and open C (C G C G C E). Other sets, like GHS' True Mediums, use the first, second, and sixth strings of a medium set and the third, fourth, and fifth of a light-gauge set. These string sets are ideal for D A D G A D and related tunings.

How about facilitating a kind of alternate tuning with a partial capo? Partial capos hold down only some of your strings and let others ring open. The Shubb partial capo, for example, can be used to cover three inside strings, such as the third, fourth, and fifth. Clamping it on at the second fret results in a D A D G A D–like Esus4 chord (E B E A B E). The Third Hand capo (Third Hand Capo Co., [207] 363-7263, www.woodpecker.com), a take-off on the old-style elastic capo, was designed to allow all possible capoing combinations. If you're not ready to go out and buy a new capo, you can use your standard spring-action capo so that it covers only strings one through five. Clamping it on in this manner at the second fret results in a kind of a fake dropped-D tuning (E B E A C♯ F♯). Kyser's Drop-D capo is specifically designed for this purpose.

If, on the other hand, you're looking for funkier gizmos to help you experiment, should check out Hipshot's Guitar Extender (Hipshot Products, [800] 262-5630, www.hipshotproducts.com), a great little tool that allows the sixth string to be lowered as far as two whole steps with the flick of a lever. The device actually replaces the sixth string's tuning peg and is available in Grover and Schaller versions. Once it has been adjusted properly and the string has been stretched, the Extender works beautifully, allowing accurate midsong retuning. Keith tuning pegs (Beacon Banjo Co., PO Box 597, Woodstock, NY 12498) work similarly, except that they can be installed in place of any or all of the guitar's tuning pegs, making possible a mind-boggling number of instant tuning combinations. These tuners were originally designed for use with the banjo and were popularized among guitarists by fingerstylist Adrian Legg.

But the ultimate retuning gadget has to be the L-CAT (TransPerformance, [970] 482-9132; www.transperformance.com). Originally designed for Jimmy Page, the system uses a set of computer-controlled electric motors to regulate the tension of each string and change tunings with the touch of a button. The touch pad gives virtually instant access to 144 preset tunings. Last but not least, there is the option of "virtually" retuning the guitar electronically via Roland's Virtual Guitar system. Used successfully by Joni Mitchell among others, the system employs a guitar synth pickup combined with a high-tech effects processor to enable any tuning and a mind-boggling number of sounds at the touch of a footswitch.

60 Tunings (and the Artists Who Love Them)

Here are 60 alternate tunings—some widely used, some one-off creations of a particular artist—along with song and artist examples. Arrows underneath tuning notes indicate strings that are altered from standard tuning and whether they are tuned up or down. Next to the notes of each tuning, you'll find the chord degree of the open strings. In dropped-D tuning, for example, if you consider D as the root (R), the other strings are the fifth (A), the root again (D), the fourth (G), sixth (B), and second (E) of a D chord, so the tuning is written as R 5 R 4 6 2. Keep in mind that sometimes the artists raise the tuning (and the key) with a capo.

Many of the songs below have been transcribed in *Acoustic Guitar* magazine; for a complete list with tunings and capo positions, searchable by song title, artist, and tuning, go to www.AcousticGuitar.com. Songs that have appeared in an *Acoustic Guitar* CD Songbook, which include complete transcriptions along with original performances on a compilation CD, are noted with the songbook title in the right column (more details on these can also be found at www.AcousticGuitar.com).

Other websites that offer valuable tuning information are www.JoniMitchell.com; www.stropes.com, which includes a database of tunings used by Michael Hedges, Leo Kottke, and others; users.plinet.com/~bquade/AlternateTuning102.html, which contains an ingenious, interactive, open-tunings chord guide; andharmony-central.com, from which you can download a couple of different alternate-tuning software programs.

SONG	ARTIST	ACOUSTIC GUITAR SONGBOOK

BASS- AND TREBLE-STRING DROPS

D A D G B E (R 5 R 4 6 2)
v

Dropped D.

And So It Goes . . .	Steve Tilston	*What Goes Around*
Arc et Senans	John Renbourn	
Beeswing	Richard Thompson	
Black Waterside	Bert Jansch	
Coryanna	Stephen Fearing	*Habits of the Heart*
A Day at the Races	Preston Reed	*Fingerstyle Guitar Masterpieces*
Durang's Hornpipe	Dan Crary	
Dust Bowl Children	Peter Rowan	
Embryonic Journey	Jorma Kaukonen	*Fingerstyle Guitar Masterpieces*
Fishing Blues	Taj Mahal	
Green Green Rocky Road	Kate and Anna McGarrigle	*High on a Mountain*
In Sorrow's Wake	Andrew York	
Jock O'Hazeldean	Martin Simpson	*Fingerstyle Guitar Masterpieces*
Living in the Country	Pete Seeger	
Look How Far	Bruce Cockburn	
Muir Woods	Andrew York	*High on a Mountain*
She's Makin' Whoopee in Hell Tonight	Lonnie Johnson	
Shotgun down the Avalanche	Shawn Colvin	
Three Quarter North	Leo Kottke	*Fingerstyle Guitar Masterpieces*
The Water Is Wide	Ed Gerhard	*Fingerstyle Guitar Masterpieces*
When You Give It Away	Bruce Cockburn	
Wondering Where the Lions Are	Bruce Cockburn	
Won't That Be a Happy Time	Joseph Spence	

C A D G B E (R 6 2 5 7 3)
v

Brother	Bill Frisell	*What Goes Around*

E A D G B D (6 2 5 R 3 5)
v

The Boxer	Paul Simon (intro/lead guitar)	

D A D G B D (R 5 R 5 6 R)
v   v

Double dropped D or D modal. Close to standard and frequently used by Neil Young.

Black Queen	Stephen Stills	
Black Water	Doobie Brothers	
Bluebird	Buffalo Springfield	
Free Man in Paris	Joni Mitchell	
Let the Bad Air Out	Bruce Cockburn	
Ohio	Neil Young	
Shelf in the Room	Days of the New	
That House	CPR	*Alternate Tunings Guitar Collection*
Use Me While You Can	Bruce Cockburn	
You Should See the Way	David Wilcox	

SONG	ARTIST	ACOUSTIC GUITAR SONGBOOK

DADGBC(26257R)

Galileo	Indigo Girls	
The Moon and St. Christopher	Mary Chapin Carpenter	*Alternate Tunings Guitar Collection*

AADGBD(RR4♭724)

The 2nd Law	Michael Hedges	*Acoustic Guitar Artist Songbook, Vol. 1*

B F♯ D G B E (R 5 ♭3 ♭6 R 4)

Embaixador	Paulo Bellinati	*What Goes Around*

D TUNINGS

DADGAD(R5R45R)

Usually referred to by its pronunciation (dad-gad), this tuning is like open D but with a suspended fourth (G) on the third string. This characterizes it as neither major nor minor. It's a favorite tuning of modern fingerstylists and Celtic rhythm guitarists.

After Your Orgasm	David Wilcox	
Barbie	David Wilcox	
Black Mountain Side	Jimmy Page	
Blow 'em Away	David Wilcox	
Catch Me if I Try	David Wilcox	
Ciara	Luka Bloom (C G C F G C)	
Dangerous	David Wilcox	
The Death of Queen Jane	Dáithí Sproule with Trian	*Alternate Tunings Guitar Collection*
Dirt Floor	Chris Whitley (C G C F G C)	
Do I Dare	David Wilcox	
From One Island to Another	Chris Whitley (C♯ G♯ C♯ F♯ G♯ C♯)	
Mary Watches Everything	Luka Bloom	
Mirage	Alex de Grassi	
Ragamuffin	Michael Hedges	
Santa Monica	Pierre Bensusan	
Snow Prince	Larry Coryell	
Soldier's Joy	Beppe Gambetta	
Spin	David Wilcox	
Strong Chemistry	David Wilcox	
Travis	Béla Fleck	*Habits of the Heart*
Western Ridge	David Wilcox (C G C F G C)	
Wild Country	Chris Whitley	

DADF♯AD(R5R35R)

Open D. Favored by blues and slide guitarists as well as many folksingers and modern fingerstylists. Sometimes referred to as Vastapol tuning after the song of the same name in open-D tuning. Related tunings: open E, E B E G♯ B E; open C, C G C E G C.

Alive in the World	Jackson Browne	
Amelia	Joni Mitchell (C G C E G C)	
Bella Donna	Peppino D'Agostino	*Fingerstyle Guitar Masterpieces*
Big Yellow Taxi	Joni Mitchell (E B E G♯ B E)	
Both Sides Now	Joni Mitchell (E B E G♯ B E)	
Center Stage	Indigo Girls	

SONG	ARTIST	ACOUSTIC GUITAR SONGBOOK
Chelsea Morning	Joni Mitchell	
Footprints	Kelly Joe Phelps	*Acoustic Guitar Artist Songbook, Vol. 1*
Freedom	Richie Havens	
Frozen in the Snow	David Wilcox	
Golden Key	David Wilcox	
If You Love Somebody	Guy Davis (C G C E G C)	*Habits of the Heart*
Indian Summer	Chris Whitley	
Kindness	David Wilcox	
Little Martha	Allman Brothers (E B E G♯ B E)	
Nothing Ever Lasts	Clive Gregson (C G C E G C)	*High on a Mountain*
One of These Things	Nick Drake	
Paris, Texas	Ry Cooder	
Police Dog Blues	Jorma Kaukonen (E B E G♯ B E)	
Prayer in Open D	Emmylou Harris	
Swimming	Pierce Pettis	*Acoustic Guitar Artist Songbook, Vol. 1*
A Tribute to Peador O'Donnell	Jerry Douglas	*Habits of the Heart*
Vigilante Man	Harvey Reid	

D A D F A D (R 5 R ♭3 5 R)
ˇ　　　ˇ ˇ ˇ

D minor.

Everything in Its Own Time	Indigo Girls	
Hard Time Killing Floor	Skip James	
John Henry	John Cephas and Phil Wiggins	*Alternate Tunings Guitar Collection*
Little Hands	Duncan Sheik	
Wishbone Ash	Peter Finger	

D A D E A D (R 5 R 2 5 R)
ˇ　　　ˇ ˇ ˇ

A close relative of open D and D A D G A D with a distinctive character from the close interval between the third and fourth strings.
Related tunings: E B E F♯ B E.

Daisy Goes a Dancing	Pat Kirtley	*Acoustic Guitar Artist Songbook, Vol. 1*
Days Go By	Duncan Sheik (E B E F♯ B E)	
That's Why I'm Laughing	David Wilcox	
Turning, Turning Back	Alex de Grassi (E B E F♯ B E)	

D A C♯ E A E (4 R 3 5 R 5 or R 5 7 2 5 2)
ˇ　　　ˇ ˇ ˇ

Rainy Road into Atlanta	Cheryl Wheeler	*Rhythms of the Road*

D A D E G C (R 5 R 2 4 ♭7)
ˇ　　　ˇ ˇ ˇ

Tattered Old Kite	David Wilcox	

D A E G A D (R 5 2 4 5 R)
ˇ　　　ˆ ˇ ˇ

Hejira	Joni Mitchell (B F♯ C♯ E F♯ B)	
My Secret Place	Joni Mitchell (C♯ G♯ D♯ F♯ G♯ C♯)	
101 South	Peter Finger	*Alternate Tunings Guitar Collection*
Slouching towards Bethelehem	Joni Mitchell	

SONG	*ARTIST*	*ACOUSTIC GUITAR SONGBOOK*

D A E F# A D (R 5 2 3 5 R)

Cherokee Louise	Joni Mitchell
Deep Lake	Bruce Cockburn (C G D E G C)
Night Ride Home	Joni Mitchell (C G D E G C)
Sunny Sunday	Joni Mitchell (C# G# D# E# G# C#)

D A D F# B E (R 5 R 3 6 2)

Will the Circle Be Unbroken	Tommy Jones

D A D G D F# (R 5 R 4 R 3)

A favorite of Nick Drake. Requires very light strings for tuning trebles up so high. Related tunings: C G C F C E and B♭ F B♭ E♭ B♭ D.

Bird Flew By	Nick Drake
Bottle of Blues	Beck (C G C F C E)
Come Away to Sea	David Wilcox (C G C F C E)
Hanging on a Star	Nick Drake (B♭ F B♭ E♭ B♭ D)
Hazey Jane I	Nick Drake
Hazey Jane II	Nick Drake (C G C F C E)
Introduction	Nick Drake
Northern Sky	Nick Drake
Pink Moon	Nick Drake (C G C F C E)
Parasite	Nick Drake (C G C F C E)
Which Will	Nick Drake (C G C F C E)

D A D G D G (R 5 R 4 R 4)

Fly	Nick Drake

D A D G A F# (R 5 R 4 5 3)

Place to Be	Nick Drake

D A C G C F (R 5 ♭7 4 ♭7 ♭3 or 2 6 R 5 R 4)

Down to the Delta	Bruce Cockburn

D A D D A D (R 5 R R 5 R)

Highway in the Wind	Arlo Guthrie
Meditation (Wave upon Wave)	Arlo Guthrie

D G D D A D (R 4 R R 5 R)

Road	Nick Drake

D D D D A D (R R R R 5 R)

A favorite of Stephen Stills.

4 + 20	Stephen Stills (E E E E B E)
Suite: Judy Blue Eyes	Stephen Stills

SONG	ARTIST	ACOUSTIC GUITAR SONGBOOK

D A E E A A (R 5 2 2 5 5 or 4 R 5 5 R R)

v   ^ v v

| All Along the Watchtower | Michael Hedges | |

G TUNINGS

D G D G B D (5 R 5 R 3 R)

v v   v

Open G. Probably the most popular tuning for slide guitar. Often called Spanish tuning, referring to the popular open-G song "Spanish Fandango." Also favored by Hawaiian slack-key guitarists, who refer to it as taro-patch tuning. Related tuning: open A, E A E A C♯ E.

Arthur McBride	Paul Brady	Alternate Tunings Guitar Collection
The Circle Game	Joni Mitchell	
Daughter	Pearl Jam	
Gertie Ruth	Roy Rogers (C F C F A C)	Habits of the Heart
Going to California	Led Zeppelin	
Let's Go to Town	Memphis Minnie and Kansas Joe	
Marcie	Joni Mitchell	
Moe 'Uhane (Dream Slack Key)	Sonny Chillingworth	Alternate Tunings Guitar Collection
Nightshift	David Wilcox	
Penny for Your Thoughts	Peter Frampton	
Rosalie	Mike Dowling	Habits of the Heart
Sangisangy	Dama	What Goes Around
Stack Lee's Blues	Steve James	Rhythms of the Road
Steamboat Gwine 'round the Bend	John Fahey	
Water Song	Jorma Kaukonen	
Vaseline Machine Gun	Leo Kottke	

D G D G B E (5 R 5 R 3 6)

v v

G6: standard except for the bottom two strings tuned down one whole step.

Angels We Have Heard on High	Mike Marshall	Acoustic Guitar Artist Songbook, Vol. 1
I Still Want To	Catie Curtis	What Goes Around
Hurricanes, Earthquakes, and Tomatoes	Doyle Dykes	Acoustic Guitar Artist Songbook, Vol. 1

D G D G B♭ D (5 R 5 R ♭3 R)

v v   v   v

G minor.

California Dreamin'	Chris Proctor	Fingerstyle Guitar Masterpieces
Dance of Death	John Fahey	
Diminished Returns	Laurence Juber	
Mist Covered Mountains of Home	John Renbourn	

D G D G A D (5 R 5 R 2 5)

v v   v v

Accordingly	Chris Whitley (D♯ G♯ D♯ G♯ A♯ D♯)	
Ghost in the Music	Nanci Griffith	

D G D F♯ B D (5 R 5 7 3 5)

v v   v   v

G major 7, G wahine. Popular among slack-key guitarists. In slack-key parlance wahine means that the tuning contains a major seventh.

Punahele	Ray Kāne	
Whee Ha Swing	Ledward Kaapana	Alternate Tunings Guitar Collection

SONG	ARTIST	ACOUSTIC GUITAR SONGBOOK

D G C G C D (5 R 4 R 4 5)
v v v   ^ v

Prelude from Bach Cello Suite No. 1   Dylan Schorer (see p. 70)

G B D G B E (R 3 5 R 3 6)
^ ^

Cinquante Six   Ali Farke Toure

F G D G B E (♭7 R 5 R 3 6)
^ v

Slow Creek   Beppe Gambetta   *Acoustic Guitar Artist Songbook, Vol. 1*

C TUNINGS

C G D G B E (R 5 2 5 7 3 or 4 R 5 R 3 6)
v v

Low C.

1952 Vincent Black Lightning   Richard Thompson

Just As I Am   Chet Atkins

Swing Low, Sweet Chariot   Duck Baker   *Acoustic Guitar Artist Songbook, Vol. 1*

C G D G B D (R 5 2 5 7 2 or 4 R 5 R 3 5)
v v   v

Like open-G tuning, but with a nice low C on the bottom. Slack-key guitarists refer to this tuning as C wahine.

Cheap Vacations	Chris Proctor
Cold Blue Steel and Sweet Fire	Joni Mitchell
Eleven Small Roaches	Michael Hedges
Golden Day	David Wilcox
Hi'ilawe	Ray Kāne
It's Almost Time	David Wilcox
Shells	Keola Beamer

C G C G C E (R 5 R 5 R 3)
v v v   ^

Open C.

Busted Bicycle	Leo Kottke	
Caledonia	Dougie MacLean	*Alternate Tunings Guitar Collection*
Eye of the Hurricane	David Wilcox	*Alternate Tunings Guitar Collection*
Foxglove	Bruce Cockburn	
Mango	David Wilcox	

C G C G C F (R 5 R 5 R 4)
v v v   ^ ^

Bourrée I and II	John Renbourn	*Fingerstyle Guitar Masterpieces*
River Rat Jimmy	Kelly Joe Phelps	*Rhythms of the Road*

C G C G C D (R 5 R 5 R 2)
v v v   ^ v

Altitude	Chris Whitley (C♯ G♯ C♯ G♯ C♯ D♯)
Amaranth	Bill Mize
Bob's Song	Martin Simpson

SONG	*ARTIST*	*ACOUSTIC GUITAR SONGBOOK*
Scrapyard Lullaby	Chris Whitley (C♯ G♯ C♯ G♯ C♯ D♯)	*Habits of the Heart*
Toth Song	Peter Lang	
Wolf at the Door	Patty Larkin	*What Goes Around*

C G C D G A (R 5 R 2 5 6)
v v v v v v

Lovely Joan	Martin Carthy	

C G D F C E (R 5 2 4 R 3)
v v v ^

A favorite of Joni Mitchell.

Coyote	Joni Mitchell	
Don Juan's Reckless Daughter	Joni Mitchell	
Just Like This Train	Joni Mitchell	
Sistowbell Lane	Joni Mitchell	
Woman of Heart and Mind	Joni Mitchell	

C F C F C F (R 4 R 4 R 4)
v v v v ^ ^

From the Morning	Nick Drake	*High on a Mountain*
Harvest Breed	Nick Drake	

C♯ G♯ C♯ F(E♯) F♯ C♯ (R 5 R 3 4 R)
v v v v v v

Loco Girl	Chris Whitley	

C G D G A D (R 5 2 5 6 2 or 4 R 5 R 2 5)
v v v v

A favorite tuning of English guitarist Dave Evans and Celtic fingerpicker El McMeen, who calls it low-C tuning.

Carolan's Dream	El McMeen	
High Hill	David Wilcox	
I Want You	Michael Hedges	
My Mary of the Curling Hair	El McMeen	
Queenie's Waltz	Adrian Legg	*Fingerstyle Guitar Masterpieces*
Show Me the Key	David Wilcox	
Silent Prayer	David Wilcox	
Star of the County Down	El McMeen	*High on a Mountain*
The Water Garden	Alex de Grassi	*Alternate Tunings Guitar Collection*

C G D G C D (R 5 2 5 R 2 or 4 R 5 R 4 5)
v v ^ v

Cullen Bay	Steve Baughman	
Donal Og/My Generous Lover/	Martin Simpson	*Acoustic Guitar Artist Songbook, Vol. 1*
The Coo Coo Bird/Santa Cruz		

C C D G A D (R R 2 5 6 2)
v ^ v v

Aerial Boundaries	Michael Hedges	

SONG	ARTIST	ACOUSTIC GUITAR SONGBOOK

E-MINOR TUNINGS

E B D G A D (R 5 ♭7 ♭3 4 ♭7)

A favorite tuning of David Crosby.

| Déjà Vu | David Crosby | |
| Guinnevere | David Crosby | |

E B E G A D (R 5 R ♭3 4 ♭7)

A close relative of D A D G A D that is used heavily by fingerstylist Peter Finger.

| Pictures | Peter Finger | |
| Tap Room | Chris Proctor | *Acoustic Guitar Artist Songbook, Vol. 1* |

E B B G B D (R 5 5 ♭3 5 ♭7)

| Not a Pretty Girl | Ani DiFranco | *Alternate Tunings Guitar Collection* |

E B B E A B (R 5 5 R 4 5)

| Robert's Serenade | Steve Baughman (see p. 78) | |

MIDDLE-STRING DROPS

E A D G A E (5 R 4 ♭7 R 5 or R 4 ♭7 ♭3 4 R)

| Caleb Meyer | Gillian Welch | |

E A D F♯ B E (R 4 ♭7 2 5 R or 5 R 4 6 2 5)

Cello Song	Nick Drake	
The Embers of Eden	Bruce Cockburn	
Isn't That What Friends Are For?	Bruce Cockburn	
Last Night of the World	Bruce Cockburn	
Mango	Bruce Cockburn	*Rhythms of the Road*
The Thoughts of Mary Jane	Nick Drake	

E A D F♯ A E (R 4 ♭7 2 4 R or 5 R 4 6 R 5)

| Gone to Santa Fe | David Wilcox | |

E A D E A E (5 R 4 5 R 4 or R 4 ♭7 R 4 R)

| Walk on J.J. Cale's Walk | Franco Morone | *High on a Mountain* |

E A C♯ F♯ B E (R 4 6 2 5 R)

| Rovin' on a Winter's Night | Scott Nygaard (see p. 75) | |

E A C♯ E A E (R 4 6 R 4 R or 5 R 3 5 R 5)

| Turning Point | David Wilcox | |

SONG	ARTIST	ACOUSTIC GUITAR SONGBOOK

B TUNINGS

B F♯ C♯ F♯ B F♯ (R 5 2 5 R 5)
v v v v ⌃

Klimbim	Don Ross	*Rhythms of the Road*

B F♯ B E A E (R 5 R 4 ♭7 4)
v v v v v

The Magdalene Laundries	Joni Mitchell	

B F♯ D♯ D♯ F♯ B (R 5 3 3 5 R)
v v ⌃ v v v

Borderline	Joni Mitchell
How Do You Stop	Joni Mitchell
Turbulent Indigo	Joni Mitchell

B♭ B♭ D♭ F A♭ B♭ (R R 3 5 ♭7 R)
v ⌃ v v v v

Black Crow	Joni Mitchell

F TUNINGS

F A D G B E (R 3 6 2 ♭5 7)
⌃

Mysterious Habitats	Scott Tennant/Dušan Bogdanović	*Habits of the Heart*

F A C G C F (R 3 5 2 5 R)
⌃   v ⌃ ⌃

The Coming Rains	Bruce Cockburn
Live on My Mind	Bruce Cockburn

NEVER MISS A BEAT

Subscribe to Acoustic Guitar

Get the #1 resource for all things acoustic guitar delivered right to your door.

EVERY ISSUE INCLUDES

- Tips on technique
- Essential gear reviews
- Sheet music for the songs you want to learn
- Interviews with your favorite players
- Lessons to help you become a better acoustic guitar player
- And more

Be the acoustic guitarist you want to be with the magazine for acoustic guitar players, by acoustic guitar players.

Sign up today!

MORE TITLES FROM STRINGLETTER

Learn authentic techniques, hone your skills, and expand your understanding of musical essentials with the help of our song and lesson books including:

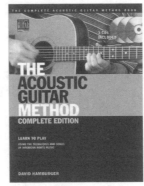